Asian Elegance

QUILTING WITH JAPANESE FABRICS AND MORE

Kitty Pippen and Sylvia Pippen

Martingale®
& COMPANY

Asian Elegance:
Quilting with Japanese Fabrics and More
© 2003 Kitty Pippen and Sylvia Pippen

That Patchwork Place® is an imprint of
Martingale & Company®.

Martingale & Company
20205 144th Avenue NE
Woodinville, WA 98072-8478
www.martingale-pub.com

Printed in China
08 07 06 05 04 03   8 7 6 5 4 3 2 1

Library of Congress Cataloging-in-Publication Data

Pippen, Kitty.
   Asian elegance : quilting with Japanese fabrics and more /
Kitty Pippen and Sylvia Pippen.
      p. cm.
   ISBN 1-56477-483-X
   1. Patchwork—Patterns. 2. Quilting. 3. Appliqué—
Patterns. 4. Textile fabrics—Asia. 5. Textile fabrics,
Hawaiian. I. Pippen, Sylvia II. Title.
   TT835.P563 2003
   746.46—dc21   2003013859

Mission Statement

Dedicated to providing quality products and
service to inspire creativity.

Credits

President: Nancy J. Martin
CEO: Daniel J. Martin
Publisher: Jane Hamada
Editorial Director: Mary V. Green
Managing Editor: Tina Cook
Technical Editor: Laurie Baker
Copy Editor: Karen Koll
Design Director: Stan Green
Illustrator: Laurel Strand
Photographer: Brent Kane
Cover and Text Designer: Stan Green

Dedications

To my loving partner, Peter, our children, Amy, Brian, and Kim, and our grandchildren, Samantha and Matthew. To my parents, Kitty and Eldon, who will always be my inspiration.
  —*Sylvia*

To my beloved twin sister, Marie Stanley.
  —*Kitty*

Acknowledgments

A heartfelt *mahalo* to Linda Kobayashi, Julie Yakamuri of Kapaia Stitchery, and Marcia King on Kauai for introducing me to Hawaiian fabric and flowers. Thank you to Elsa Bakalar, my garden and writing mentor, to my brother David for his computer expertise, and to the Boots family, Linda Driscoll, and Nelson Shifflett for their encouragement and support.
  —*Sylvia*

My sincere thanks for the continued support of my many students, family, and friends, and especially my daughter Sylvia, who has expanded my horizons with her Polynesian quilts.
  —*Kitty*

Heliconia with Bamboo
by Sylvia Pippen, 31" x 38".

This quilt was inspired while gardening on Hanalei Bay beneath a stand of lobster-claw heliconias and bamboo. The two-foot flower heads hung like waxy jewels overhead among huge spade-shaped leaves; perfect for appliqué as well as cascading bouquets. Paper-pieced batiks were used to capture the blended colors of the petals and bamboo leaves. Sashiko outlines the bamboo. This quilt won Best in Class at the 2002 Marin Quilt and Needle Arts Show.

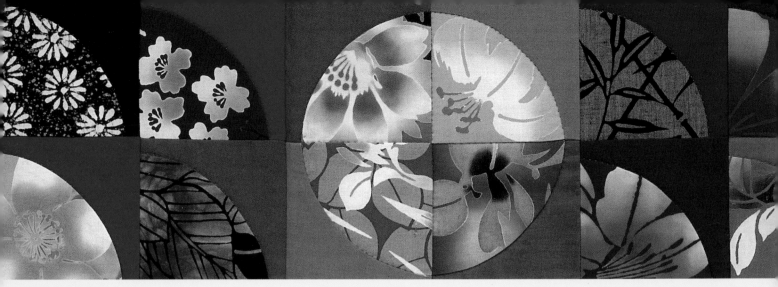

Contents

From the Authors

Celebration 80 by Kitty Pippen, 40" x 46".

The Japanese silk used in this mosaic-type quilt was a birthday gift from my children. Each piece of the small and large medallions was backed with paper and appli-quéd to the dark background. Snowflake designs on the background fabric inspired sashiko quilting using four strands of embroidery floss. The quilt won first place and Best in Class at the 2000 Marin Quilt and Needlework show.

*I*N MY WILDEST DREAMS I NEVER THOUGHT I would write another book. However, when I realized my daughter had become very interested in quilting, it sparked the idea of co-authoring a mother-daughter work. Also, I felt confident about tackling the daunting idea because Sylvia agreed to take on the writing. That left me free to make more quilts!

Students often ask how I came to make quilts of Asian fabrics. Raised by missionary parents in the mountains of rural China, I learned the joy of working with my hands and developed a life-long appreciation for Asian design. Many years later, I discovered authentic Japanese kimono fabric in the San Francisco Bay area, where we lived. I embarked on my first quilt, a huge king-size quilt named "Cranes." The recognition I received for that quilt was a great incentive to continue working with Japanese fabrics. The quilt turned out well, but I don't recommend taking on such a large quilt for a first project!

I want to share with you my enthusiasm and appreciation for Japanese and Asian textiles and design. Throughout these pages, I hope to introduce you to exquisite Japanese fabrics such as yukata, kasuri, and kimono silk. Other fabrics, such as batiks, marbled silk, and wool, blend beautifully with them.

From years of experimenting, I have developed different designs and construction techniques that I hope will help you use your stash of fabrics in innovative ways. Many of my quilts now are appliquéd, based on mathematical principals, and my work has become more colorful as I have departed from predominately Japanese indigo blues. I have also been influenced by my daughter's Polynesian-style quilts and her fearless use of bright colors.

—*Kitty Pippen*

*T*HREADS RUN THROUGH GENERATIONS. My mother, Kitty, has been my creative inspiration from the time I could hold a needle or pair of scissors. I would sew right along with her, making doll blankets as she braided rugs from a rainbow of wool tweeds and solids. She taught me to sew and introduced me to the world of quilting. Coauthoring a book with my mother is an honor, and I hope to articulate her quilting wisdom. I have had the benefit of one-on-one Kitty Pippen workshops all my life and am happy to repay the debt by being the "pen" for our book.

Just as my mother's quilts are influenced by her life in China, my quilts took on a tropical twist when I moved to Hawaii. After living through twenty-five New England winters, I was captivated by the beauty of Hawaii and island culture. I was compelled to express my love affair with the tropics through my quilts.

I also discovered Kapaia Stitchery, a one-of-a-kind quilt store on Kauai stocked with fabric that reflects Hawaii as a cultural crossroad: Hawaiian aloha shirts and bark cloth reproductions, French-Polynesian pareu, Japanese yukatas, American-made Japanese prints, and batiks. Many of my quilts evolved from my fabric finds.

My quilts are not replicas of traditional Hawaiian or South Pacific quilts; they are adaptations that use Polynesian designs, motifs, and fabrics. Understanding the cultural context that influences my quilts has greatly enhanced my creative process. Polynesia has a rich quiltmaking tradition that expresses the intimate relationship islanders have with their environment. Exposed to woven cloth little more than 200 years ago, Hawaiians and South Pacific Islanders have developed unique whole-cloth and appliqué quilts that reflect the vibrant plants and colors of Polynesia and their centuries-long tapa textile tradition.

***Orchid Tivaevae* by Sylvia Pippen, 50½" x 50½".**

Tifaifai, also spelled tivaevae, is a traditional Cook Island bedspread. This quilt was inspired by a quilt designed by Ruta Tixier Rarotong and was featured in The Art of Tivaevae: Traditional Cook Islands Quilting by Lynnsay Rongokea. The stylized leaf patterns and cattleya orchids were appliquéd and then embellished with chain stitch, French knots, and whipstitch embroidery. Cotton solids were used except on the throat of the orchid, which is batik. The scalloped border is appliquéd. In contrast to Hawaiian quilts, tifaifai are usually backed but not sandwiched with batting.

Through these pages, I hope to inspire you to make quilts using the exuberant images and fabrics of the tropics.

—*Sylvia Pippen*

Japanese Designs and Fabrics

JAPAN IS A NATION OBSESSED BY TEXTILES. The love of fabric links all the decorative arts and the kimono, the national costume and a symbol of great beauty.

The kimono has a long history, reflecting influences from the cultures of India, China, Korea, and Southeast Asia. Early textile history of Japan is misty, but archaeologists have determined that prior to 300 BC, wood or vegetable fibers, also called blast fibers, were used to make fabric. There is also evidence that silk was used when Japan began to trade with two of its neighbors, China and Korea.

Another important development in the field of textiles was the import of cotton from China and Korea in the fifteenth century. The plant flourished in Japan and was valued because it provided greater warmth than the blast fibers. Two other valuable imports came from trade with China and Korea: clothing from China, including the basic kimono form, and the Buddhist religion, which had tremendous influence in Japanese art and textiles.

During many centuries, domestic unrest and civil war went hand in hand with prosperity and cultural development. Japanese merchants became wealthy, and as the standard of living rose, they demanded more elaborate clothing, leading to the development of more ornate textiles.

Although quiltmaking in Japan is a comparatively new phenomenon, all the elements—quilting, patchwork, and appliqué—have been present in this part of the world for centuries. The Japanese traditionally sleep on a stab-stitched or tied channel-quilted quilt laid on the floor, called a futon, and they pull another quilt over themselves. This type of padded futon, often beautifully decorated, was the ancestor of our modern quilts, which Japanese women make so enthusiastically today.

ELEMENTS OF DESIGN

Whether it is a painting, sculpture, or piece of fabric, you can count on nature to play a role in traditional Japanese design. The Japanese have a profound appreciation of nature, and each motif taken from nature has symbolic meaning. For instance, pine, bamboo, plum blossom, and chrysanthemum represent the four seasons. You may find these motifs from nature used alone or intertwined with other traditional Japanese objects, such as fans, boats, bundles of ribbons, and bridges.

Geometric details are also often found in Japanese designs. Circles, hexagons, and diamonds may fill background space, or they may be used to outline or contain other designs.

Nature and geometry also play parts in the manner in which elements are arranged. Because nothing in nature is perfectly balanced or symmetrical, you will see designs off center, overlapping, or even disappearing over the edge of a composition. Designs are often arranged on the diagonal, an element you'll see in many Japanese works of art.

Space around the design is often as important as the motifs. Movement is created by scattering patterns or by placing designs off center within shapes such as hexagons, squares, or fans. And when designs overlap or are cropped, the viewer must reach into his or her imagination and determine the rest of the design.

JAPANESE FABRICS

Japanese fabrics come in the form of a *tan*, a roll of cloth 14½" wide by 14' long—just the right amount for constructing a kimono. Textiles are highly valued in Japan, and kimonos are often saved and handed down from generation to generation. Valuable kimonos are taken apart, washed, and reassembled when they become soiled. Many of our quilts are made with new materials as well as old hand-sewn kimonos that have been ripped apart.

The following discussion and photographs will introduce you to some fabrics of Japanese origin. They are becoming more widely used in American quilts, and more American fabric retailers are incorporating them into their selection.

Indigo

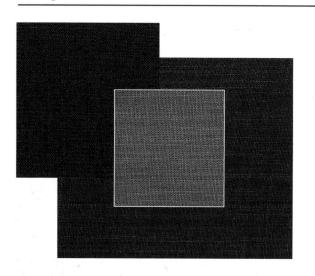

Indigo fabrics have been used traditionally for Japanese and Chinese clothing. The indigo dye is made from a variety of plants. Leaves are cut, dried, and composted to promote fermentation. The dye is stored in vats that are buried in a clay floor and kept at a constant temperature. It is a long process to make a vat of dye, and the cloth dipped in each vat may produce a different shade of indigo. Deeper shades may be achieved by dipping the cloth multiple times. Natural indigo dyes continue to bleed whenever the fabric is washed. For this reason, we recommend using an indigo-colored fabric that has been dyed using a chemical process if you want to incorporate it into a design with yukata (see page 12) or American-made fabrics.

White sashiko worked on dark indigo is a beautiful combination. You can see an example of this in "Ginkgo—Signs of Good Fortune" shown below.

Ginkgo—Signs of Good Fortune
by Kitty Pippen, 32" x 51".

The ginkgo-leaf yukata was purchased many years before I had the courage to cut into it. While I was trying to figure out how I would use it, I decorated some indigo squares with sashiko in a variety of ginkgo leaf designs. Finally, with the addition of some red-and-white kasuri and a piece of blue *katazome*, I was able to put the quilt together in a satisfying arrangement.

Kasuri and Ikat

Kasuri is one of the most fascinating Japanese fabrics because of the many steps involved in making it. Threads of the warp and the weft are marked with resist, a substance that resists dye, before they are dyed and woven. Each length of thread from selvage to selvage has a different marking. The resulting designs have characteristic fuzzy edges. The dragon, sky, and cranes in "Night of the Dragon" below and the butterfly in "Ginkgo—Signs of Good Fortune" on page 10 were made using this method. Kasuri is usually sold as single panels.

Ikats are also made with resist-marked threads, but many of the steps are done by machine. Ikats are marked to create geometric designs and are traditionally used for men's kimonos. Try using them in your quilt borders to create excitement and movement.

Night of the Dragon
by Kitty Pippen, 46" x 59".

The central piece in this quilt is the big kasuri dragon. Other kasuri designs make up the quilt, but the most valuable and treasured one is the sky fabric. It was designed and woven by Mr. Tanaka, a well-known textile designer I visited in Japan. Mr. Tanaka won awards for this fabric. The quilt was shown in the 2002 Pacific International Quilt Festival.

Yukata

One of the most useful fabrics for quilting is yukata because it is soft, lightweight, and easy to needle. Yukata patterns vary from blue-and-white geometrics, used for men's clothing, to colorful florals, used for women's garments.

The designs on yukata are made by the *kata-zome* method, which involves dyeing through a stencil. Because the dyes penetrate the material, there is no right or wrong side. This makes reversing directions of a design possible.

Large, bold yukata designs combine well with smaller designs and are useful for all kinds of quilts. You can see how they were used in "Linked Shapes Sashiko Panel" (page 23), the "Scrappy Yukata" detail at right, and "Ginkgo—Signs of Good Fortune" (page 10).

Silk

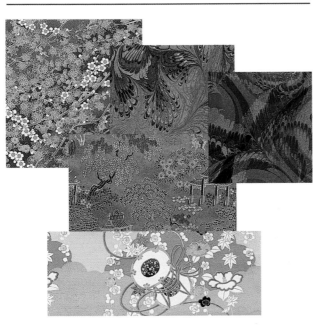

Silk is one of the finest and most beautiful natural fibers. The Japanese and Chinese weave shantung, crepe, and brocade fabrics from silk yarns. These fabrics all work well for appliqué. American-made marbled silk is also very useful in quiltmaking. Raw silk, which has a nubby texture and stable weave, is good for use as a background.

Many quilters avoid using silk because it is rather difficult to handle. To overcome the tendency of silk to shimmy and slip, try using the paper-piecing method for appliquéing pieces. This involves basting the fabric over a paper pattern to help stabilize the piece. The detail from "Notre Dame Rose," shown below left, and "Celebration 80" on page 6 were made using this method.

American-Made Japanese Fabric

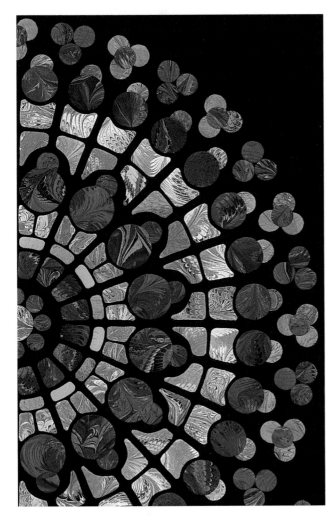

American fabric stores carry many cotton fabrics with Japanese-inspired prints. Designs include traditional Japanese motifs, such as fans, bamboo, cranes, and cherry blossoms. Because these fabrics are three times as wide as traditional Japanese yukata, they have many motifs to work with. These fabrics may be used to make any of the projects in this book.

Polynesian Designs and Fabrics

COMBINING ELEMENTS OF POLYNESIAN culture with American quiltmaking has created unique blended art forms that echo the evolution of the islands. The quilts of the Hawaiian, Society, and Cook Islands are each as distinctive as the islands they represent.

Many of the islands of the Pacific, especially the Hawaiian Islands, are very isolated geographically. Thousands of years ago, before the influence of Western or Eastern culture, a sophisticated nonwoven cloth tradition called tapa, or *kapa* in Hawaii, evolved. Tapa, also known as bark cloth, was made from strips of the paper mulberry tree that were pounded and sewn or glued together to make a large sheet of cloth, then stamped or painted with geometric or leaf designs. From this cloth, the Hawaiians made kapa quilts, using the silky wool that covers the *hapu'u pulu* tree fern for "batting" and sewing the layers together with bone needles.

In contrast to Japan or China's long woven textile history, woven cloth arrived on the islands of Polynesia only when Captain Cook arrived in the late 1700s. In the early 1800s, missionaries sailed to all parts of Polynesia, bringing bolts of calico cotton, steel needles, and trunks of quilts. Quilts were hardly needed for warmth, but the missionaries nonetheless taught the native islanders their patchwork and appliqué techniques. The islanders took up appliqué, developing patterns that echoed their ancient tapa designs. They may also have been influenced by the missionaries' Baltimore Album quilts and snowflake-style designs of *scherenschnitte*, a German paper-cutting technique.

The whole-cloth appliqué quilt, most often associated with Hawaii, became a popular art form throughout the islands, perhaps born of practicality. Fabric that had traveled around the horn was a precious commodity, and the island quilters thought it was a waste to cut a bolt of turkey-red calico into little pieces for patchwork. Only the northerly Hawaiians made traditional sandwiched quilts, while South Pacific islanders made *tifaifai* bedspreads that had no batting but were backed with a single piece of fabric.

ELEMENTS OF DESIGN

Polynesian quilts throughout the islands are an extension of the quilter's natural and spiritual world. A quilt is not simply an individual's artistic interpretation; it is full of hidden symbolic meaning deeply rooted in the culture. Even with many diverse styles among the islands of Polynesia, there are common quilt design elements: nature and spiritual motifs, symmetry, contrast, and repetition with variation.

The islanders draw upon their own backyards for inspiration. Flowers and plants are a vital part of the island culture and are the essence of most quilt designs. Hibiscus, orchids, and pikake are common motifs, along with breadfruit, palm leaf, and ferns. The striking beauty of a place, often associated with an event, can inspire a quilt. For example, Na Molokama, the name of streams that flow through Hanalei Valley, Kauai, is interpreted in a quilt pattern that echoes tumbling water through green ferns. The quilt designs of Hawaii are the most highly stylized and do not attempt to depict nature realistically, but are meant to evoke spiritual connections by leaving interpretation up to the viewer. Patterns and names of quilts often carry private meanings known only to the quiltmaker.

The art of designing a quilt on folded cloth or paper is a highly regarded skill throughout the Pacific Islands. Most women use a paper pattern for cutting an appliqué design, but some brave souls with a vision can cut freehand directly into cloth.

In contrast to Japanese design, symmetry is basic to all Polynesian quilt patterns. Hawaiians cut their quilt patterns from one piece of fabric folded into eighths and then cut as you would a paper snowflake; the South Pacific islanders fold their quilt patterns into fourths. Residents of all of the islands make whole-cloth quilts, as well as quilts cut from separate pieces of fabric that are arranged around a central medallion. Hawaiian quilters usually use two contrasting colors, but the South Pacific islanders use three or more fabrics for their tifaifai.

Contrast is very important in Polynesian quilt design, and usually a darker foreground is appliquéd onto a lighter background. Often the form of a design is varied slightly, but the color themes remain the same. For example, one of the most popular designs, "Tahitian Flower," is varied by portraying the little white jasmine flower in different stages: bud, half open, and/or in full bloom.

POLYNESIAN FABRICS

Walking into a Hawaiian fabric store is a feast of island imagery; bolts of cloth display sunsets with swaying palms, hula dancers, plumeria leis and hibiscus, Asian tigers, Mount Fuji, and ancient Polynesian geometric tapa designs. Not for the faint-of-heart, the colors of Tahitian pareu, tropical aloha, and bark-cloth prints are dazzling, the patterns big and bold. The motifs of these tropical island fabrics are a synthesis of Asia and Polynesia and offer quilters a bright, daring new dimension.

Aloha Tropical Prints

The tropical prints of Hawaii evolved to supply the demand for "aloha" shirts, the wearable "postcards" worn by visitors and locals alike. The fabric for aloha shirts has its roots in the cultural mix of Honolulu, where many Chinese and Japanese pineapple and sugarcane laborers turned to the more profitable art of tailoring. The first shirts were modeled after the utilitarian loose cotton Philippino *palaka* shirt. Dry-goods stores supplied the fabric: summer-weight cotton yukata and silks from Japan, batik and rayon from the US mainland. In the mid-1930s, Hawaiian clothing manufacturers decided to produce cloth that was uniquely Hawaiian in design.

Pareu

***Floating Plumeria* by Sylvia Pippen, 25½" x 35".**

Weddings on the beach and trade winds often blow plumeria into Hanalei Bay. The contrast of alabaster petals against turquoise water inspired this quilt. The petals are needle-turned appliqué. The border was a serendipitous addition found in my mother's stash.

In Tahiti, around 1810, lightweight printed cotton, called pareu, was imported from England. Draping easily, pareu replaced traditional tapa cloth as a body wrap. Originally the pareu cotton was hand painted with tapa dyes. Later the pareu was printed with solid blue, deep red, and green backgrounds with big white floral motifs, such as breadfruit or hibiscus. These wraps became very popular and are featured in the paintings of Tahitians by Paul Gaugin. The Tahitian and Samoan pareus influenced the designs used in the budding garment industry in Hawaii in the mid 1930s. In addition to the traditional wrap, pareu fabric is used for everything from curtains and hula costumes to car-seat covers and, of course, quilts.

Bark Cloth

Bark cloth, or cretonne, was originally imported from France in the 1920s. Americans dubbed it bark cloth because of its nubby texture. It is a loosely woven cotton fabric that has two weights; light clothing-weight lava cloth and heavier bark cloth used for upholstery and curtains. The lush tropical prints were influenced by art deco and were wildly popular in Hawaii and the mainland during the 1930s through the 1950s. Bark cloth is enjoying a renaissance today with many irresistible reproductions available.

Hawaiian Linked Shapes
by Sylvia Pippen, 38½" x 49".

Linked shapes is a traditional Japanese sashiko pattern. Reproductions of Hawaiian vintage bark cloth were used for the triangles, and the hexagons were assembled using the English paper-piecing method. The hexagons are embellished with sashiko tropical flowers.

Batiks

Batiks make a wonderful addition to any quilt. The colors available span the rainbow in gradated hues and are perfect for tropical flower petals and stained glass appliqué. Most batiks have a high thread count and are particularly good for small appliqué projects because the dyeing process the fabric undergoes renders a fabric that remains stable and doesn't fray. Batiks also are a perfect secondary fabric when used with large tropical prints.

Washington National Cathedral West Rose Window by Sylvia Pippen, 33" x 33".

On a visit to the National Cathedral, the afternoon sun illuminates the West Rose Window. The abstract design of the stained glass in this quilt was created using mottled and marbled batiks. Each segment of the stained glass was paper pieced and appliquéd onto a cotton sateen background. To make the dark leading recede and the stained glass shapes puff up, I quilted each piece in the ditch after layering.

Appliqué Techniques

ᴍᴀɴʏ ᴏꜰ ᴛʜᴇ ǫᴜɪʟᴛꜱ ɪɴ ᴛʜɪꜱ ʙᴏᴏᴋ feature appliquéd elements. We have chosen to hand appliqué the motifs using one of the three methods presented here. Each project specifies the type of appliqué method that we used to make the quilt, but it is ultimately up to you whether you choose one of these methods or another method that you are familiar with. Just be sure to make the necessary modifications if you want to use a different method than the one indicated.

In general, we recommend the paper-piecing method for precise geometric designs, such as the squares in "Spiraling Squares" on page 40, and the needle-turn method for free-form shapes, such as the leaves and flowers of "Tahitian Hibiscus" below and on page 70. Freezer-paper appliqué is used primarily for "snowflake" appliqué designs, such as "Hawaiian Panel" on page 66. These designs get their name from the way the design is cut out; a piece of paper is folded in fourths, and then one quarter of the design is traced onto it. When the paper is cut on the traced lines and the paper unfolded, the full pattern emerges, much like the snowflakes many of us first learned to cut in grade school.

"Tahitian Hibiscus" quilt detail illustrates the needle-turn method for free-form shapes of leaves and flower petals.

PAPER-PIECING METHOD

Perfectly formed shapes are achieved in this method by hand basting the seam allowance around the edges of a paper shape.

1. Trace the appliqué pattern(s) onto typing paper the number of times indicated in the project instructions for each shape. Cut out the shape(s). Take care to trace and cut accurately; every bump will show on your finished appliqué shape. Do not add seam allowances when tracing the appliqué shape onto the paper.
2. Write the corresponding pattern number on the wrong side of each paper shape so you can keep track of how each piece fits into the design.
3. Pin each paper shape to the wrong side of the appropriate fabric, positioning each one on the bias. It is much easier to turn a bias edge around a curve. Cut around each shape, adding a generous ¼" seam allowance all around.

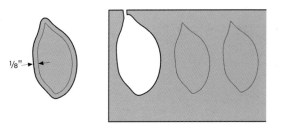

¼" seam allowance

Wrong side of fabric

4. Fold the ¼" seam allowance onto the paper (back) side of each shape. Clip seam allowances only where necessary, such as on the inside of a tight curve. Baste around the edge of each shape through all the layers.
5. Refer to "Traditional Appliqué Stitch" on page 22 to appliqué each shape in place where indicated in the project instructions.
6. Remove the basting stitches. Make a small slit in the background fabric behind the appliqué and remove the paper shape.

NEEDLE-TURN METHOD

Needle-turn appliqué proceeds directly from cutting the piece to appliquéing it onto the background fabric.

1. Trace each appliqué pattern onto template plastic and cut it out.
2. Place the template(s) on the right side of the appropriate fabric(s). Trace around each template with a fine-line ink pen. Trace as many of each shape as indicated in the project instructions.

Plastic template

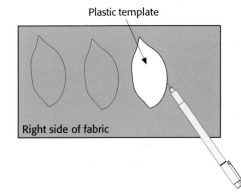

Right side of fabric

3. Cut out each appliqué shape, adding a ⅛" seam allowance all around.

⅛"

4. Referring to the project instructions, position the first appliqué on the quilt top. Pin the shape in place, or baste it in place, placing the basting line well within the marked line so the seam allowance can be turned under completely.

5. Using the tip of the needle, gently turn under a short length of seam allowance, making sure the marked line is not visible. Refer to "Traditional Appliqué Stitch" below right to stitch down the turned-under portion. Continue turning under and appliquéing short sections until the entire shape is appliquéd.

6. Repeat steps 4 and 5 to position, baste, and appliqué the remaining shapes in place in the order indicated.

FREEZER-PAPER METHOD

This method works especially well for small "snowflake" appliqué quilts. To help prevent the edges from raveling, the pattern is marked on cloth and basted to the background fabric before the design is cut away.

1. Referring to the project instructions, cut a piece of freezer paper the size indicated. Fold the paper into quarters, dull side out, and trace the pattern onto it. Be sure the fold lines on the paper match up with the pattern fold lines or the design will not emerge as one piece.
2. Cut out the pattern and unfold it. With the glossy side down, iron the freezer-paper pattern onto the right side of the appropriate fabric.
3. Trace around the pattern, using a fine-tip permanent ink pen. Remove the pattern from the fabric.
4. Place the marked appliqué fabric over the background fabric, positioning the traced design so it is in the correct position on the background.
5. Baste the appliqué to the background fabric inside the marked lines of the motif.
6. Cut away the appliqué fabric ⅛" beyond the marked line removing only a small section at a time. Refer to "Needle-Turn Method" on page 21 to turn the seam allowance under and appliqué in place. Continue cutting away small amounts of the appliqué fabric beyond the marked lines, turning under the seam allowance, and appliquéing it in place until the entire shape is appliquéd.

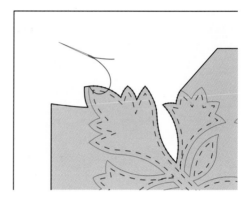

TRADITIONAL APPLIQUÉ STITCH

The trick to impeccable appliqué is to make your stitches invisible. Use a sharp, fine appliqué needle and 60-weight machine quilting thread or extra-fine thread, such as silk, that exactly matches the appliqué fabric. Beginning on a straight edge, insert the needle into the background fabric underneath the appliqué piece. Come up through the background fabric, just catching the edge of the appliqué. Be sure to push the needle into the background fabric directly below your last stitch and slightly under the appliqué piece. Stitches should be no more than ⅛" long. Give the thread a slight tug every five to six stitches.

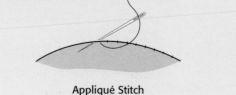

Appliqué Stitch

Sashiko

$\mathcal{S}$ASHIKO IS A FORM OF QUILTING THAT USES a heavier contrasting thread to emphasize the design. It may be worked through all three layers of a quilt, but it is easier to work through a single layer as an embellishment.

Patterns for sashiko vary widely. Stylized geometric shapes are based on horizontal, vertical, or diagonal lines, or on circles. Motifs from nature, such as ocean waves, clouds, bamboo, tortoise shells, flowers, lightning, and cranes appear frequently. In addition to nature motifs, sashiko can be innovative meandering designs. We have included several patterns at the back of this book for your use. You can enlarge or reduce them to fit your design.

Traditional Japanese sashiko thread is usually white, soft, and thick and looks very striking on a dark background, such as indigo. However, sashiko thread may be too thick to use on lighter-weight fabrics. Embroidery floss, #8 perle cotton, and silk thread are alternative choices; select the one that works best for the fabric you are embellishing.

Linked Shapes Sashiko Panel
by Kitty Pippen, 13" x 40".

The interlocking geometric design came from *Sashiko: Blue and White Quilt Art of Japan* by Kazuko Mende and Reiko Morishige. Traditional white sashiko thread was used to stitch the design on Japanese indigo fabric. The borders of the panel are kasuri decorated with cranes.

23

"Ginkgo—Signs of Good Fortune" detail

The sashiko designs are family crests stitched with heavy white thread on Japanese indigo.

MARKING A SASHIKO DESIGN

There are several ways you can transfer a sashiko design to a dark fabric. To use a light box, place the sashiko pattern on the light box, lay the fabric on top, and trace the design lines directly onto the fabric with a white marking pencil. If the fabric is very dark and the lines are difficult to see, it sometimes helps to place a second copy of the pattern in the same size alongside your work as a reference. Another way to transfer a design is with dressmaker's carbon. Place the pattern on the fabric, slip a contrasting color carbon in between, carbon side down, and go over all the lines with a fine lead pencil. Use the white marking pencil to tidy up the lines on the indigo itself. If a sashiko design has only a few simple elements or curves, you might trace the entire design onto template plastic, cut out the individual shapes, and trace around them. Make sure all your final lines are fine and free from smears in order to provide the ideal guide for neat, smooth stitches.

STITCHING A SASHIKO DESIGN

Once you've mastered sashiko, you may want to try it for background quilting in place of Western patterns. To emphasize the beauty of these patterns, try quilting them with colored threads or metallics. After you've experimented on quilts, try sashiko on garments, pillows, and table runners. It adds much richness to the surface design. Here's how to do the basic stitch.

1. Cut a 20" to 24" length of sashiko, thread it onto a sharp needle with a large eye, and make a small, single knot at the other end. Plan your stitching route so that it does not require too many twists, turns, or long skipping spaces on the back.

2. Bring the threaded needle up from the back of the marked fabric. By placing the point of the needle flat on the line a short distance from the point at which the thread emerges, it is possible to measure the first, second, and third stitches before drawing the thread completely through the fabric. You want all the stitches to be the same length, ideally five to seven stitches per inch. If the needle is angled or held straight up before making a stitch, the point may not stay on line or you may misjudge the stitch length.

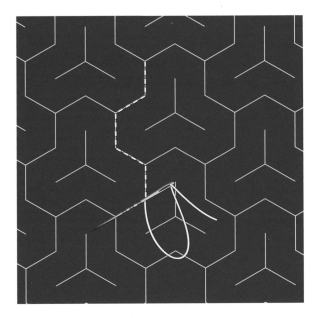

3. After stitching for an inch or two, pull up on the thread a little, and then, using a thumbnail, stretch out the stitching. The idea is to keep the work loose—especially the thread on the back—so that the stitching does not pucker.

SASHIKO TIPS

Traditional sashiko instructions provide detailed directions regarding the stitching routes to take and the number of stitches per leg of the design, but as you acquire experience and confidence, you will develop your own methods. The main concern is to keep the stitches even and the lines smooth. Here are a few tips:

- A stitch must end at the turn of a corner, either with the thread going to the back or coming up to the top.

- To stitch a very small circle or a sharp, tight curve, it may be necessary to make the stitch on the back smaller than on the front.
- Threads that skip across the back should not measure longer than ½". Sometimes a longer skip can be avoided by weaving the thread through several stitches on the back to reach a new section of the marked design.
- To finish off a line of stitching, pull the threaded needle through to the back, and weave the thread tail through several stitches before clipping the tail. Resume stitching with a newly knotted thread.

Finishing Techniques

YOUR BEAUTIFUL QUILT TOPS DESERVE TO be finished so they can be displayed and enjoyed. The instructions here will show you how to make the quilt sandwich, baste and quilt the layers together, and then bind the edges.

SANDWICHING AND BASTING

Cut the quilt backing a few inches larger than the quilt top, piecing it if necessary. A quilt hangs best if the backing seam is centered, or if two seams are placed at equal distances from the side edges.

Iron the quilt top and backing. Spread the backing wrong side up on a flat surface, such as a bed or table. Center the batting over the backing, and then add the quilt top, right side up. Keep the edges of the quilt top parallel to those of the backing if possible.

Carefully slip a large poster board under the center of the quilt sandwich. Pin together the sandwiched layers in this area, and then thread baste in two directions, making rows of stitching 4" to 5" apart. Remove the pins as you baste an area together. Keep the basting stitches no longer than ½". Begin with a knotted thread, and end by fastening securely; your basting stitches may need to remain in place for a long time, depending upon how fast and often you quilt.

Continue pinning and basting the quilt layers together. To reposition the poster board, gently lift the sandwich and move the board under another section. Once all the areas on your work surface are basted, it is safe to reposition the entire sandwich and move any overhanging edges to the surface for basting. Finish with short basting stitches ¼" in from the edge all around the perimeter of the quilt top. Trim the batting to within ½" of the edges of the quilt top so that it will not stretch or snag while you work. Don't forget to remove all of the pins!

QUILTING

Most quilters enjoy this phase of the quiltmaking process. After hours of exacting design and construction and the rather mundane job of basting, the work takes on a new dimension.

Quilting can be done with or without a hoop or frame. Unless the quilt is very large, we prefer to work with the quilt in our lap and do not use a hoop or frame. If a quilt is very large, we may spread it out on a table or another large flat surface to gain access to the area we want to quilt. To keep the quilt backing flat and wrinkle free, we lift and smooth the sandwich from underneath, between basting lines, and anchor all the layers with a straight pin. We can then quilt up to the pin, move it to another spot, and continue.

Because we have basted very carefully, we can begin quilting anywhere on the quilt. To initially stabilize and anchor the work, we quilt in the ditch (right along the seam) around pieced blocks and appliqué, and next to sashing strips and borders. There is one exception, however. We quilt ¼" from seams that are pressed open.

After stabilizing the quilt, we quilt around the largest designs and motifs, such as leaves and petals, and along any stems. We then quilt background areas with traditional sashiko patterns: pointed waves, clamshells, intersecting circles, basket weaves, or fret designs (see page 88 for patterns). Areas of actual sashiko also require some quilting unless the sashiko itself has been worked through all three thicknesses of the quilt. It is usually enough to stitch right beside some of the lines of sashiko stitching. Borders can then be filled with a variety of complementary designs, including variations of those described above, or with echo quilting to mimic meandering clouds or lines of water or wind.

BINDING AND FACING

We use two methods to finish the edges of our quilts: binding and facing. A binding will show on both the front and back of the quilt, whereas a facing is turned entirely to the back. Both methods are described here, although all of the projects in this book are bound.

For either approach, begin by measuring and jotting down the quilt dimensions. Iron the quilt front and back, and trim the batting and backing even with the quilt top. If trimming loosens or removes the basting around the edge of the quilt, take time to redo it.

Binding

All binding strips should be cut 2" wide on the straight of grain unless otherwise indicated.

1. Cut two binding strips the length of the vertical measurement of the quilt and two strips the horizontal measurement plus 1" to allow for a finished corner. If you must join strips for a longer length, sew an angled seam to prevent excess thickness at the spot where the binding is turned.
2. Press the binding strips in half lengthwise, wrong sides together.

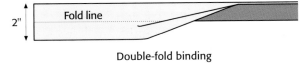

Double-fold binding

3. With the raw edges matching, pin the side binding strips to the quilt front. Stitch, using a ¼" seam allowance.
4. Fold the strips to the back of the quilt so that the binding fits snugly around the raw edges. Hem stitch the folded edge in place.
5. Add the top and bottom binding strips in the same manner, leaving an equal amount of

excess at each end. Fold back the excess at each end to overlap and conceal the side binding strips when the binding is hem stitched in place.

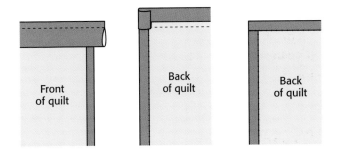

Facing

This method incorporates the sleeve into the facing, which works well for small quilts. For larger, heavier quilts, or to protect the back of a very valuable quilt, construct the sleeve as a tube in the more traditional manner.

1. Cut two straight-grain strips 2" or 3" wide and the length of the quilt top. The width will depend on the size of the quilt and your personal preference.
2. With right sides together and raw edges matching, stitch each side strip to the quilt top, using a ¼" seam allowance. From the front side of the quilt, press the strip away from the seam line. (Use a pressing cloth for dark colors.) Topstitch ⅛" from the seam through all the layers.

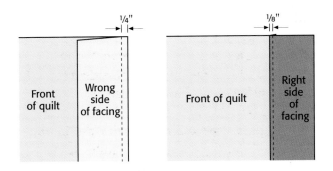

3. Turn the quilt over. Fold the facing onto the back of the quilt, making sure a tiny edge of the quilt top rolls to the back. Press as you go, using quite a bit of steam. Turn the raw edge under and hem it to the back of the quilt.

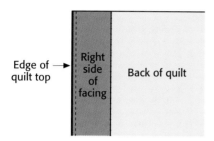

4. Cut the facing for the bottom edge 2" or 3" wide and 1" longer than the quilt width to allow for a finished corner. Turn the quilt to the front side. With right sides together, stitch the bottom facing to the bottom edge of the quilt, making sure the strip extends ½" beyond the quilt at each end.

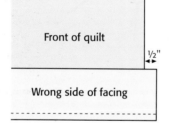

Topstitch, fold back, and press the bottom facing as you did for the sides. Fold in the excess at each end and hem in place.

5. For the top edge facing, which will also serve as a hanging sleeve, cut the strip 5" wide and 2" longer than the quilt width. With right sides together, sew the facing to the front top edge, allowing a 1" extension at each end. Topstitch as before.

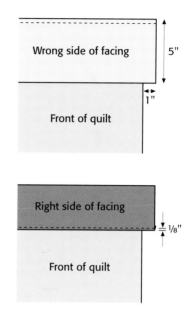

6. Fold the 1" extensions to the back of the facing strip and tack in place. Fold the facing to the back of the quilt, pressing well. Fold under and hem the long edge; then stitch the hemmed edge to the quilt back. Leave the ends open so you can insert a dowel for hanging the quilt.

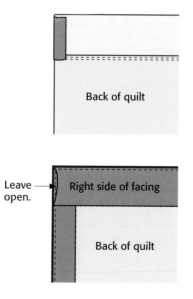

Notre Dame Rose
by Kitty Pippen,
35" x 53".

This quilt was inspired by a trip to Paris where I visited the Notre Dame Cathedral. From pictures of the rose window, I was able to design the quilt. Marbled silk, made by Marjorie Lee Bevis, was used for the mosaic. Each piece was backed with typing paper and appliquéd to the dark background. After the quilt was sandwiched, each shape was quilted in the ditch to make the dark spaces recede and the silk puff up. The quilt won first place at the 2000 Marin Quilt and Needlework Show and second place at the 2000 Pacific International Quilt Festival IX.

From Asia with Love by Kitty Pippen, 27" x 27".

Twelve 6" mosaic squares made of precious Japanese silk scraps were just enough to fit around a 12" square of silk with the Chinese character for love appliquéd on it.

Japanese Flower Carts
by Kitty Pippen, 19" x 44".

The Japanese associate the wheel with good fortune, and so we see it used on many art objects and kimonos. It is also a popular design motif for traditional Japanese embroidery.

Marbled Silk Mosaic by Kitty Pippen, 42" x 44".

This was inspired by a book on Japanese optical and geometric art. Marbled silk was used for the preformed paper-backed appliqué pieces. Quilting in the ditch helps bring the silk appliqué into relief.

Silk Hexagon and Triangle Panel
by Kitty Pippen, 15" x 32".

Colorful Japanese silk hexagons were sewn to shantung silk triangles.

Plumeria with Sashiko
by Sylvia Pippen, 16" x 32".

Plumeria, or frangipani, is the essence of Hawaii captured in a flower. First brought from India, plumeria trees are found in every garden and are used to make exquisitely fragrant leis. The plumeria are made using the paper-piecing method and appliquéd with a contrasting thicker edge to give the illusion of a fluted petal. Movement is created in the water with sashiko.

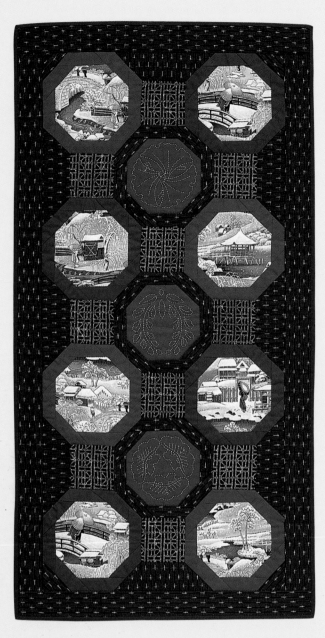

Silent Snow Scene
by Kitty Pippen, 22" x 42".

The charming little Japanese houses and people in this American-made fabric inspired this quilt. Each framed octagon shows a different snow scene. The quilt was machine pieced and quilted by hand.

Linked Hydrangeas
by Kitty Pippen, 32" x 42".

A collection of beautiful yukata fabrics decorated with hydrangeas inspired this quilt. Hexagons and equilateral triangles fit together perfectly if the side of the hexagon is one-third the length of the side of the triangle. All sorts of interesting arrangements can be designed on isometric grid paper. To make the quilt, I paper pieced all the patches and whipstitched them together by hand. After the paper was removed, I appliquéd the pieced blocks to an accent border and then sewed it to a wide blue border by machine. The charm of the quilt is the interesting irregular border and the diagonal placement of the fabric designs.

Tranquil Waters
by Kathleen Swick, 23½" x 25½".

Yukata fabric is enhanced with sashiko in this wall hanging. Appliquéd hexagons were added to represent bubbles, and more sashiko motifs embellish the borders.

Hawaiian Octagon
by Sylvia Pippen, 24" x 35".

Framed octagons picture Hawaiian women gathering fruit, fish, and flowers. Plumeria and anthurium are outlined in sashiko. A bamboo print is used to complement the large pictorial design. The quilt was machine pieced and hand quilted.

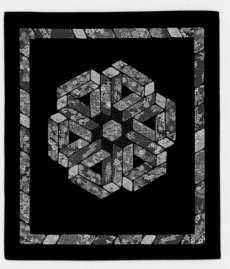

Optical Illusion by Kitty Pippen, 29" x 33".

The idea for this little quilt came from a Dover publication, *Triad Optical Illusions* by Harry Turner. To make this mosaic-type quilt, Japanese *chiremen* silk was basted over paper shapes and appliquéd to an indigo background.

Art Nouveau by Kitty Pippen, 39" x 50".

The idea for this quilt came from several books of art nouveau. It is definitely a departure from my usual Japanese-looking quilts. Four different shades of marbled blue silk were appliquéd to a background of raw silk.

**Sashiko and Silk Hexagon
by Kitty Pippen, 36" x 41".**

Making a silk mosaic out of a geometric sashiko design was quite a challenge. The kimono silk was a gift from a friend and because there was a limited amount of it, I used every scrap to make the border. Small versions of the large medallion were worked with sashiko in the corners.

Radiance
by Cathy Erickson, 40" x 22½".

The quilt is made of yukata with baskets of traditional Japanese autumn flowers. The quilting patterns incorporate traditional Japanese patterns and chrysanthemum family crest symbols. The quilt was recently displayed at the Seattle Asian Art Museum at a Contemporary Quilt Art Association exhibit.

Tribute to Mr. Hama
by Kitty Pippen, 36" x 41".

Mr. Hama is a talented textile designer whom I visited while I was in Japan. I met his family and saw the studio where he designs and cuts very intricate stencils to make *katazome* fabric. Mr. Hama used small touches of burned orange in his blue-and-white fabric. I was lucky to find an exact match for my border trim. My quilt was designed on isometric graph paper. The hexagons and triangles were sewn together by machine.

From China with Love by Kitty Pippen, 19" x 24".

From China with Love

The Chinese character for "love" in this quilt has a special meaning for my twin sister and me. It was part of our names as we were growing up in China: my Chinese name translates to "Loving Flower" and hers to "Loving Truth." Our good friend Betty Rockwell gave me the beautiful Chinese brocade from which the windowpanes in this quilt were cut. She had intended to make a dress from it many years ago; the pattern was still pinned to the fabric! I was overjoyed with the gift and soon made this little piece. The character background is raw silk but the sashing bars are cotton.

Finished Quilt Size: 19" x 24"

MATERIALS

Yardage is based on 42"-wide fabric.
- 1 yard of black solid for appliqués, sashing, borders, and binding
- ½ yard of batik or floral for windowpanes
- 12" x 14" rectangle of white or very light-color solid for "love" character background
- ¾ yard of fabric for backing
- 22" x 27" piece of low-loft batting
- 1 sheet of typing paper

CUTTING

All measurements include ¼"-wide seam allowances.

From the batik or floral, cut:
    4 rectangles, 3½" x 5" (A)
    2 rectangles, 3½" x 5½" (B)
    2 rectangles, 3½" x 6" (C)
    2 rectangles, 3½" x 8½" (D)
    1 rectangle, 4" x 9" (E)

From the black solid, cut:
    3 strips, 1" x 42"; crosscut into:
        6 strips, 1" x 3½"
        1 strip, 1" x 9"
        2 strips, 1" x 14"
        2 strips, 1" x 16"
    2 strips, 2" x 19"
    2 strips, 2" x 21"
    3 strips, 2" x 42"

From the backing fabric, cut:
    1 rectangle, 21" x 26"

APPLIQUÉING THE "LOVE" CHARACTER

1. Press the white 12" x 14" rectangle. Use your favorite method to center and transfer the "love" character on page 39 to the rectangle right side.
2. Trace appliqués 1–10 on page 39 onto typing paper and cut out. Mark the number on the back of each piece.
3. Referring to "Paper-Piecing Method" on page 21, pin each paper appliqué piece to the wrong side of the remaining black fabric. Cut out each shape, adding a generous ¼" seam allowance all around. Fold the seam allowance of each appliqué piece onto the paper and baste in place. Remove the pin and press each piece as you complete the basting.

4. Using black thread and working in alphabetical order, appliqué each piece to the appropriate position on the marked rectangle from step 1. As you finish each piece, remove the basting stitches, turn the rectangle over, cut a small slit in the fabric behind the appliqué, and carefully remove the paper pattern.

5. Press the appliquéd rectangle from the back. Keeping the design centered, trim the rectangle to 9" x 10".

ASSEMBLING THE QUILT TOP

1. Stitch the A, B, C, and D rectangles and the black 1" x 3½" sashing strips together as shown. Make two of each.

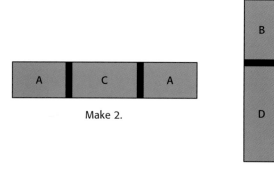

Make 2.

Make 2.

2. Stitch the appliquéd rectangle, the E rectangle, and the black 1" x 9" sashing strip together as shown. Stitch a black 1" x 14" sashing strip to each side.

3. Stitch the units from steps 1 and 2 and the 1" x 16" sashing strips together as shown below.

4. Stitch a black 2" x 21" strip to the sides of the quilt top. Sew a black 2" x 19" strip to the top and bottom edges of the quilt top. Press the finished top from both the front and back.

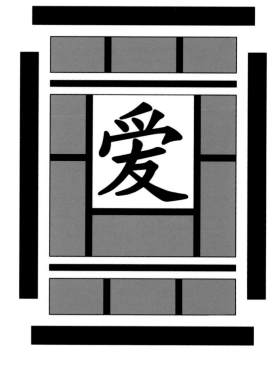

FINISHING

Refer to "Finishing Techniques" on pages 26–28.

1. Layer the quilt top with batting and backing; baste.

2. With white thread, quilt in the ditch around each appliqué piece of the "love" character. Quilt a crosshatch pattern in the space around the character. Using thread to match the windowpane fabric, quilt in the ditch on each side of the sashing and inside edge of the borders.

3. Use the black 2" x 42" strips to bind the quilt edges.

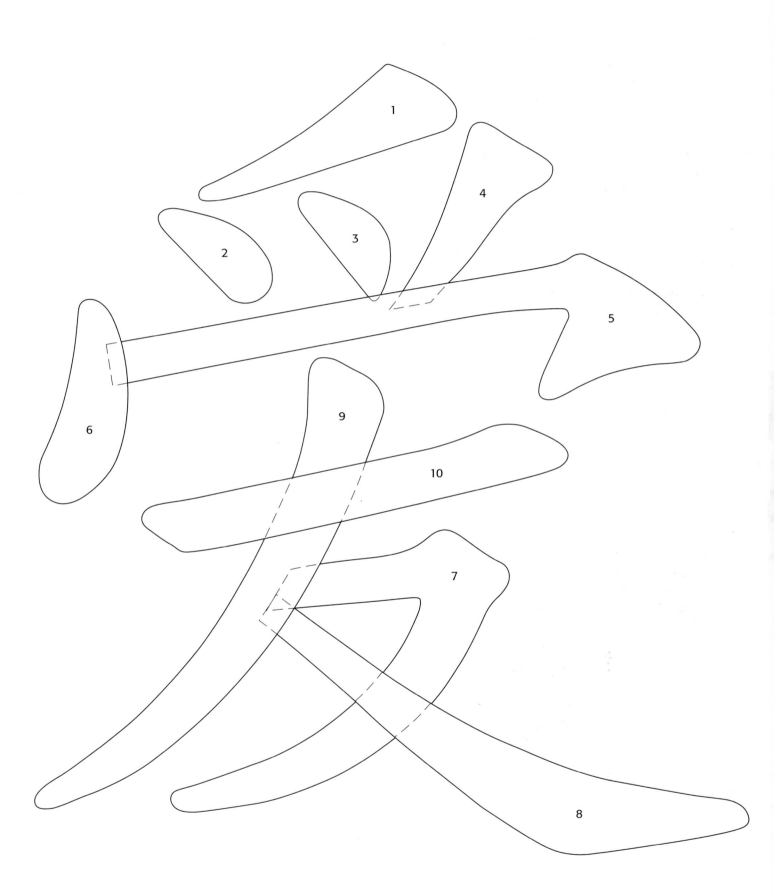

Spiraling Batik Squares by Kitty Pippen, 28" x 28".

Spiraling Batik Squares

After solving the geometric problems I encountered when making two spiraling square quilts out of silk, one of which you can see on page 45, I was ready to make one out of cotton. The multiple colors in the batik resulted in an interesting design and I decided to use it for a class project.

Finished Quilt Size: 31" x 31"

MATERIALS

Yardage is based on 42"-wide fabric.
- 1½ yards of multicolor batik for appliqués, border, and binding
- ¼ yard of coordinating batik for appliqués and border
- 28" x 28" square of dark solid for background
- 1 yard of fabric for backing and sleeve
- 33" x 33" piece of low-loft batting
- 8½" x 11" piece of template plastic
- 6 to 7 pieces of typing paper
- Chalk wheel or white chalk pencil

CUTTING

All measurements include ¼"-wide seam allowances.

From the multicolor batik, cut:
    6 strips, 2" x 42"; crosscut two strips into four strips, 2" x 16½"

From the coordinating batik, cut:
    8 strips, 2" x 10"

From the backing fabric, cut:
    1 square, 33" x 33"

PREPARING THE BACKGROUND

1. Make sure the background square is a perfect square.
2. Fold the square in half vertically and horizontally; press the fold lines. Mark the center point with a dot, using the chalk pencil. Baste on the fold lines, using a light-color thread.
3. Trace the circle patterns on pages 46 and 47 onto typing paper and cut them out.
4. Place the segmented paper circle over the background square, matching the centers. To match the centers exactly, insert a pin through the center of the paper circle so that it meets the center point of the fabric square. Be sure to do this with a cutting board or magazine under the fabric. Match the vertical and horizontal lines on the circle with the basted fold lines on the fabric. Anchor the pattern to the fabric with a few pieces of tape.

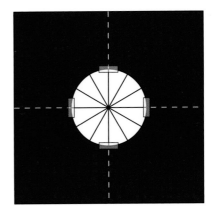

5. Align a long ruler with one of the circle's radial lines. Using the chalk wheel or pencil, extend the line onto the fabric. Repeat to extend all of the lines as shown. Remove the pattern and complete the lines through the circle.

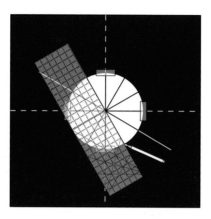

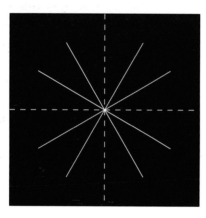

6. Beginning at the center, baste about 12" of each chalk line.

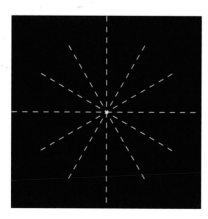

7. Center the small paper circle over the basted lines, matching the centers as described earlier. Chalk-mark around the circle pattern; then baste over the line.

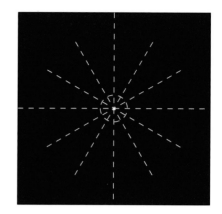

PREPARING THE APPLIQUÉS

1. Referring to "Paper-Piecing Method" on page 21, trace squares A–E on page 47 onto template plastic and cut out. Using the templates, trace 12 squares of each size onto typing paper and cut out. Write the letter on the back of each square as you go.

2. With the letter face up, pin three of each size square to the remaining coordinating batik fabric. Pin the remaining paper appliqué pieces to the wrong side of the remaining multicolor batik fabric. Cut out each square, adding a generous ¼" seam allowance all around. Fold the seam allowance onto the paper and baste in place; be sure the corners are square and the straight edges are crisp. Remove the pins and press each piece as you complete the basting.

APPLIQUÉING THE QUILT TOP AND ADDING BORDERS

1. Using thread to match the appliqués, appliqué the A squares around the basted circle perimeter, positioning the squares as shown. As

you finish each square, remove the basting stitches, turn the quilt over, cut a small slit in the fabric behind the appliqué, and carefully remove the paper pattern.

2. Position the B squares between two A squares as shown, using the basted radial lines as a guide. Appliqué the squares in place, removing the basting stitches and paper patterns as described earlier as you finish each square. Working in alphabetical order, continue appliquéing the squares to the background in this manner, using the previous squares and basted lines as placement guides.

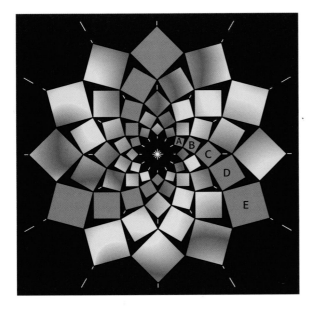

3. Press the quilt top from the front and back. If necessary, trim the top to make it square.

4. To make the pieced border strips, stitch a coordinating batik 2" x 10" strip to each end of each multicolor batik 2" x 16½" strip as shown. Trim ¼" from the stitching lines. Make 4.

5. On the wrong side of the quilt top, mark the center of each edge with a sharp pencil or pin. Also mark ¼" in from each edge at the corners. Fold each border strip in half widthwise to find the center; mark with a sharp pencil or pin.

6. Pin one border strip to one side of the quilt top, matching the centers. Transfer the quilt top corner marks to the border strip. With the border strip on top, sew from one ¼" corner mark to the other, backstitching at each end. Repeat for the remaining border strips, being sure to position each border strip so that the short edge of the multicolor strip is closest to the quilt top edge. Press the seams toward the borders.

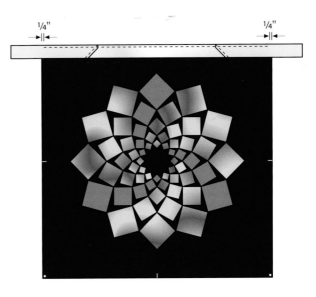

7. To make the miter, fold the quilt top in half diagonally, right sides together, matching raw edges of the border strips and extending the excess borders outward. Using a ruler with a 45° angle, draw a line on the wrong side of the border strip from the ¼" mark to the outside edge as shown. Pin the border strips together along the drawn line. Stitch directly on the drawn line.

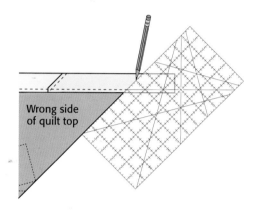

8. Turn the mitered corner right side up and make sure the points match and the corner lies flat with no puckers. Trim the seam to ¼", and press it to one side.

9. Repeat steps 7 and 8 for each of the remaining corners.

FINISHING

Refer to "Finishing Techniques" on pages 26–28.

1. Layer the quilt top with batting and backing; baste.

2. Using thread that matches the background of the quilt top, quilt in the ditch around the two sides of each A square that faces the center of the circle. Repeat for squares B, C, and D. Quilt completely around each E square. This will make the squares stand out and the spaces between them recede. Quilt the background with any geometric design, using the patterns on page 91 if desired.

3. Add a hanging sleeve. Use the remaining multicolor batik 2" x 42" strips to bind the quilt edges.

Variation

Spiraling Squares with Fans by Kitty Pippen, 37" x 37".

It was my good fortune to be given a silk kimono and a tan of wool that were both decorated with fans. My fascination with geometric designs led me to make this quilt. With the help of a ruler, compass, protractor, and chalk pencil, I marked guidelines for positioning the squares. The diagonal distance between opposite corners of any square is the length of the side of the next larger square. If this rule is followed, the squares become larger and fit together perfectly as they progress to the outer circles. To make uniform squares, the silk was backed with paper before being appliquéd to the backing. The wide border is wool.

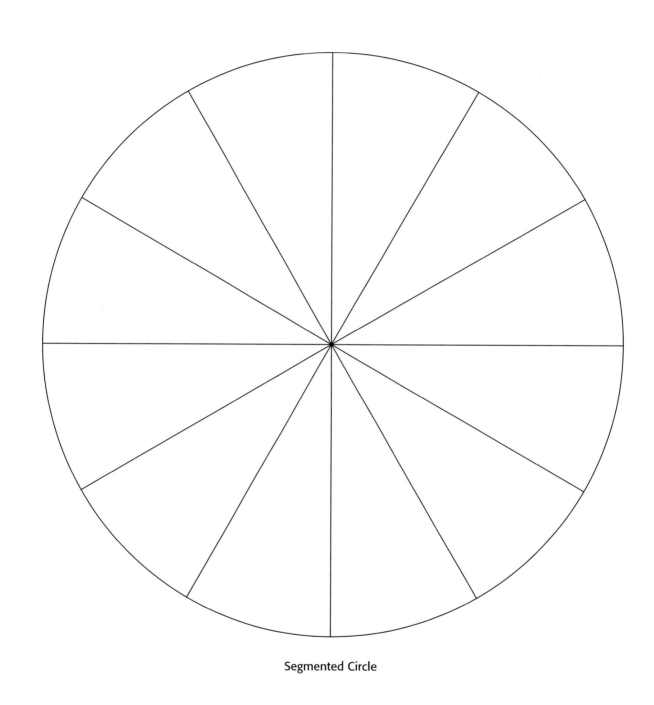

Segmented Circle

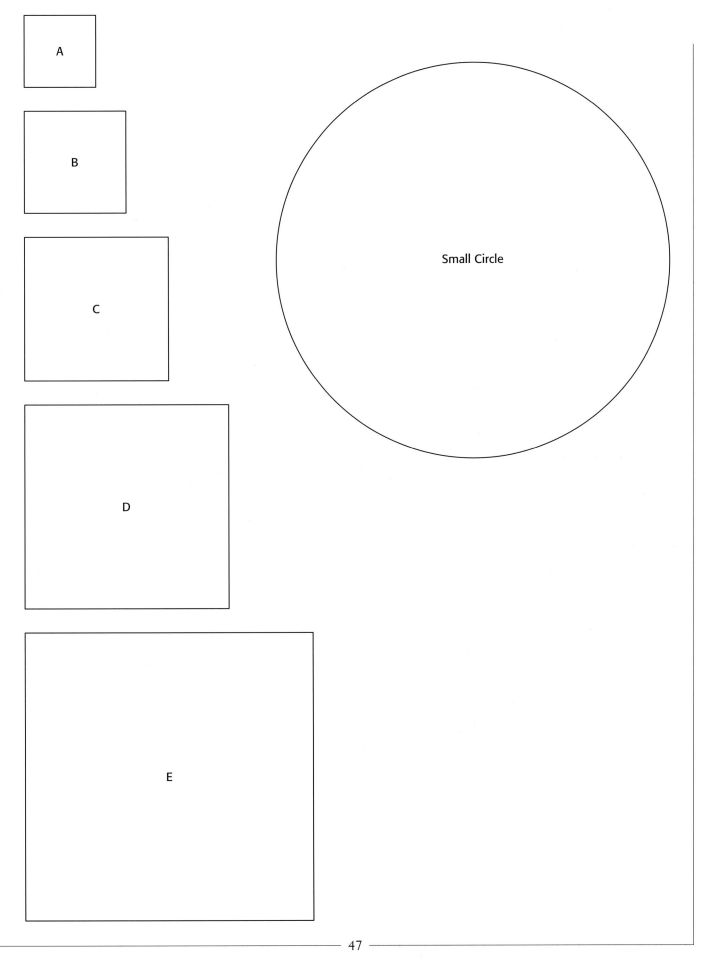

A

B

C

D

E

Small Circle

Springtime Dogwood by Kitty and Sylvia Pippen, 36" x 49".

Springtime Dogwood

Each part of this quilt has symbolic meaning in Japanese art. The chevrons represent hawk feathers, the pair of mandarin ducks brings marital bliss, and the boughs of dogwood, when hung in the rafters of a new house, prevent fire. One could imagine that the columns of the chevron piecing are sky scrapers, the background for a city park filled with dogwood trees and colorful ducks on a pond.

Finished Quilt Size: 32" x 40"

To make construction easier, the cut width and length of the strips have been changed slightly from the original. This results in a wall hanging that finishes smaller than the quilt pictured.

MATERIALS

Yardage is based on 42"-wide fabric.
- 6 to 8 fat quarters of assorted dark-color striped fabrics with the stripes running parallel to the selvage for hawk feathers
- 1½ yards of muslin for background
- ½ yard of variegated pink-and-white batik for flowers
- ¼ yard total of various green fabrics for flower centers and leaves
- ⅜ to ⅞ yard of brown fabric for branches*
- Scraps of light brown, dark brown, rust, white, gray, green, black, blue-gray, and blue—or other colors of your choosing—for ducks
- 1½ yards of fabric for backing and sleeve
- ⅝ yard of blue stripe fabric for binding
- 36" x 44" piece of low-loft batting
- Several sheets of typing paper

*Yardage amount depends on whether you cut each branch segment individually or as one whole unit.

CUTTING

All measurements include ¼"-wide seam allowances.

From each of the assorted striped fat quarters, cut:
   6 strips, 3" x 18", with the stripes running the length of the strip

From the muslin, cut:
   9 strips, 2 ½" x 42"
   1 strip, 4 ½" x 40"

From the blue stripe for binding, cut:
   2"-wide bias strips

ASSEMBLING THE BACKGROUND PANEL

1. Randomly stitch several different stripe strips together along the long edges, staggering the ends 2½" as shown. The number of strips in the unit does not matter because you will be able to adjust the length after the bias strips are cut from the unit. Make another unit with

the same amount of strips, staggering the strips in the opposite direction. Use different fabrics in each unit to give the chevrons more variety. Cut as many 2½"-wide bias strips from each piece as possible.

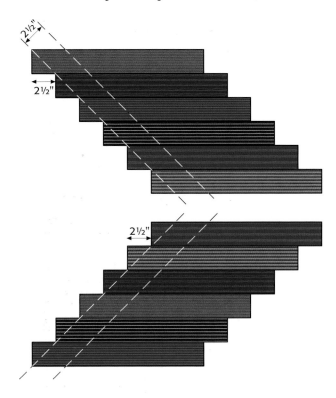

2. The bias strips will become the chevron portion of the hawk-feather strips. Depending on the amount of strips you used to make each unit, your strips may be exactly the desired length, or you may need to sew strips together or delete pieces to achieve the desired length. Using the bias strips from one unit and referring to the background assembly diagram on page 51, make the chevron portion of one hawk feather strip, adding or deleting as necessary. Use the diagram as a guide only; you do not need to make your strips exactly as

shown. Repeat to make a mirror-image strip the same length, using the bias strips from the second unit.

3. With right sides together, sew a muslin strip to the ends of each of the chevron strips as shown. Trim away the excess muslin from the seam allowances.

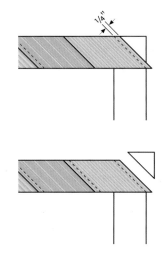

4. Referring to the background assembly diagram below for guidance only, trim away enough muslin strip from each end so that the finished strips measures 40". Stitch the strips together, matching the chevron points at each end.

5. Refer to step 1 to make additional chevron strips as necessary for the remaining six hawk feather strips, and to steps 2–4 to assemble the strips.

6. Stitch the hawk feather strips and the 4½" x 40" muslin strip together as desired, using the background assembly diagram for guidance. Press the seams in one direction.

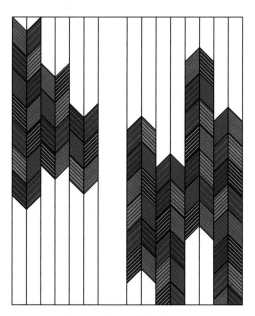

Background Assembly Diagram

APPLIQUÉING THE QUILT TOP

1. Trace the tree-branch appliqué patterns (A and B) on pages 53–57 onto typing paper. Cut out the patterns.

2. At this point, you may tape the branch patterns together and cut one large piece from the brown fabric, or cut each individual piece from brown fabric; the flowers and leaves will cover where individual pieces meet. As you cut out the piece(s), add ⅛" seam allowance all around.

3. Referring to "Needle-Turn Method" on page 21, appliqué the branch to the background panel, following the branch placement diagram.

Branch Placement Diagram

4. Trace the leaf patterns (C–E), the flower petal patterns (F–K), and the duck patterns (L–JJ) on pages 58 and 59 onto typing paper. Trace a total of 50 of C–E, 68 of F, 20 of G, 3 each of H–K, and 2 each of L–JJ. You may need more or fewer of the leaf and flower petal pieces, depending on how full you want the tree.

5. Referring to "Paper-Piecing Method" on page 21, pin each paper appliqué piece to the wrong side of the appropriate fabrics. Cut out each shape, adding a generous ¼" seam allowance all around. Fold the seam allowance of each appliqué piece onto the paper and baste in place. Remove the pin and press each piece as you complete the basting. Also cut several narrow bias strips from the remaining brown fabric for the twigs.

FINISHING

Refer to "Finishing Techniques" on pages 26–28.

1. Layer the quilt top with batting and backing; baste.
2. Quilt in the ditch around some of the flowers and branches. Use the cloud and water patterns on pages 93 and 94 to quilt the muslin portions of the background with matching thread if desired.
3. Trim the edges of the quilt, if necessary, to square it up.
4. Add a hanging sleeve. Bind the quilt edges.

6. Using matching thread, arrange four flower petals together as shown on page 58 and appliqué to the branches as desired. Appliqué the center piece (G) in place. As you finish each piece, remove the basting stitches, turn the rectangle over, cut a small slit in the fabric behind the appliqué, and carefully remove the paper. Use the brown bias strip to add various lengths of twigs to the branches and needle-turn appliqué them in place. Appliqué the leaves to the twigs and flowers as desired, removing the paper after appliquéing each piece. Add or delete flower, twig, and leaf appliqués as desired.
7. Referring to the photo on page 48, transfer the duck appliqué patterns on page 58 and 59 to the background using your favorite method. Working in alphabetical order, appliqué the duck pieces in place. Remove the paper from each piece as you finish it.
8. Press the quilt top from the wrong side.

Branch A

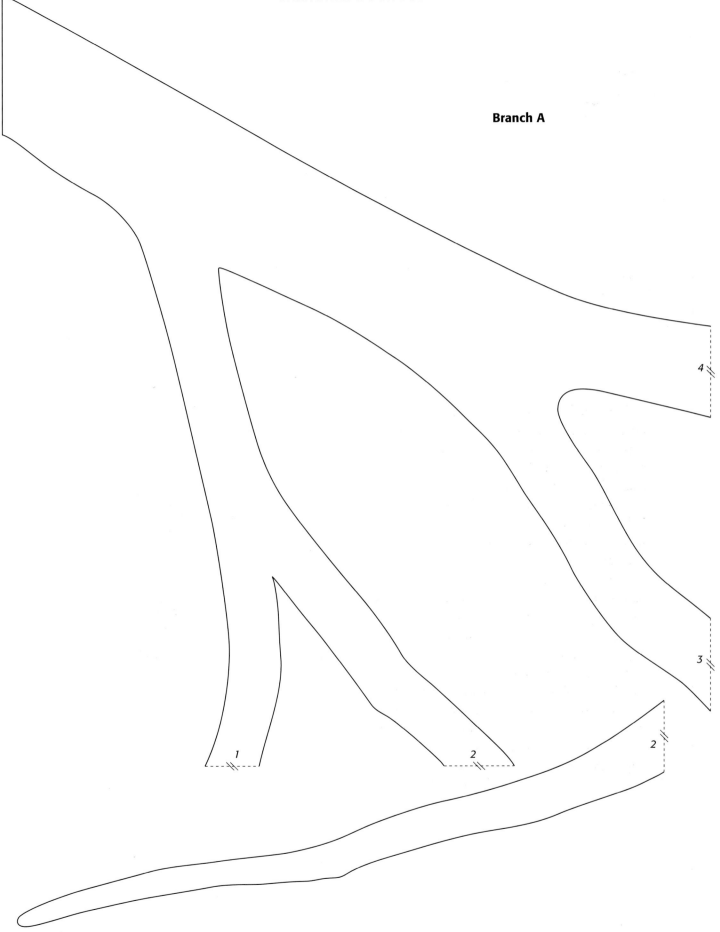

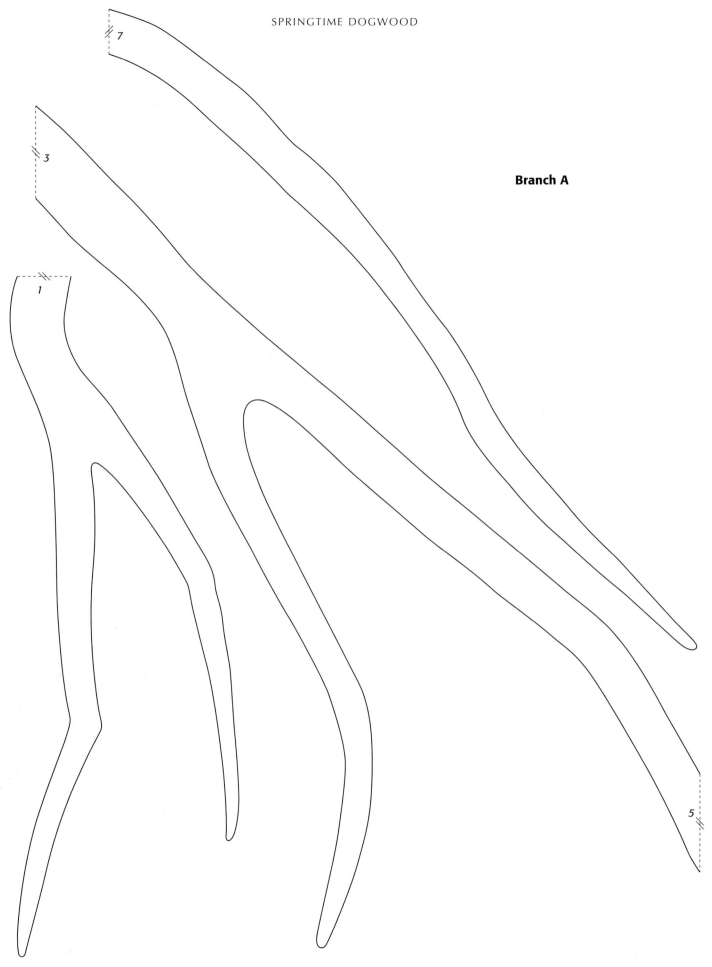

Branch A

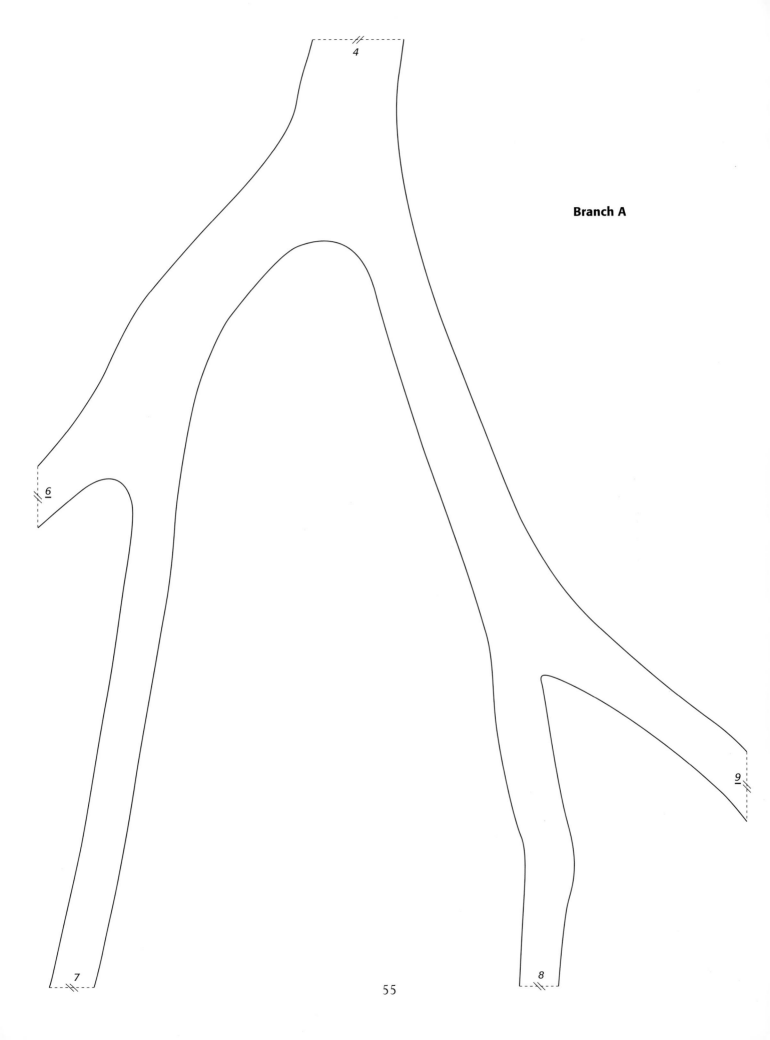

Branch A

4

6

7

8

9

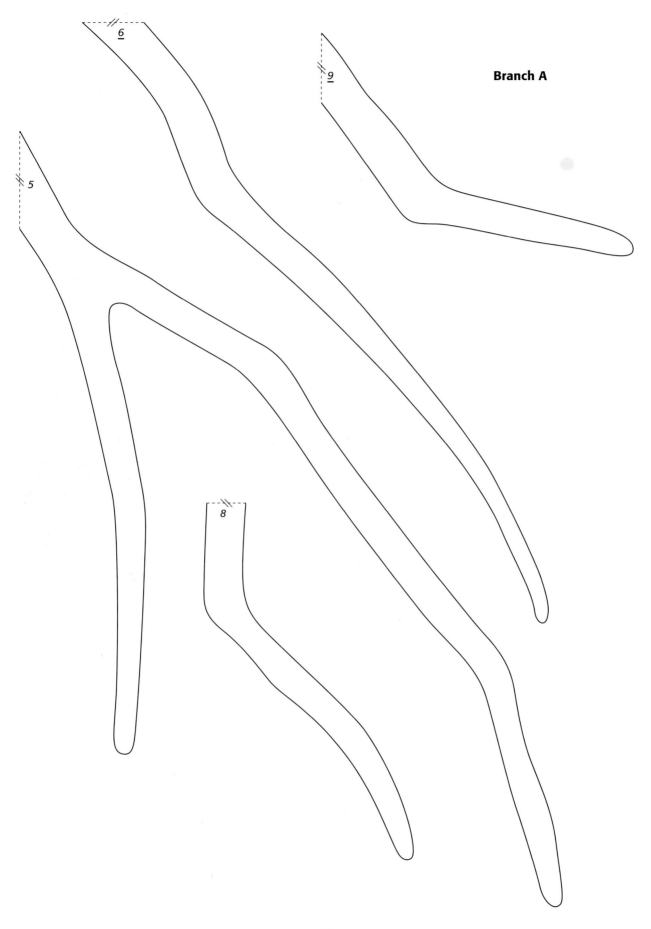

Branch A

Branch B

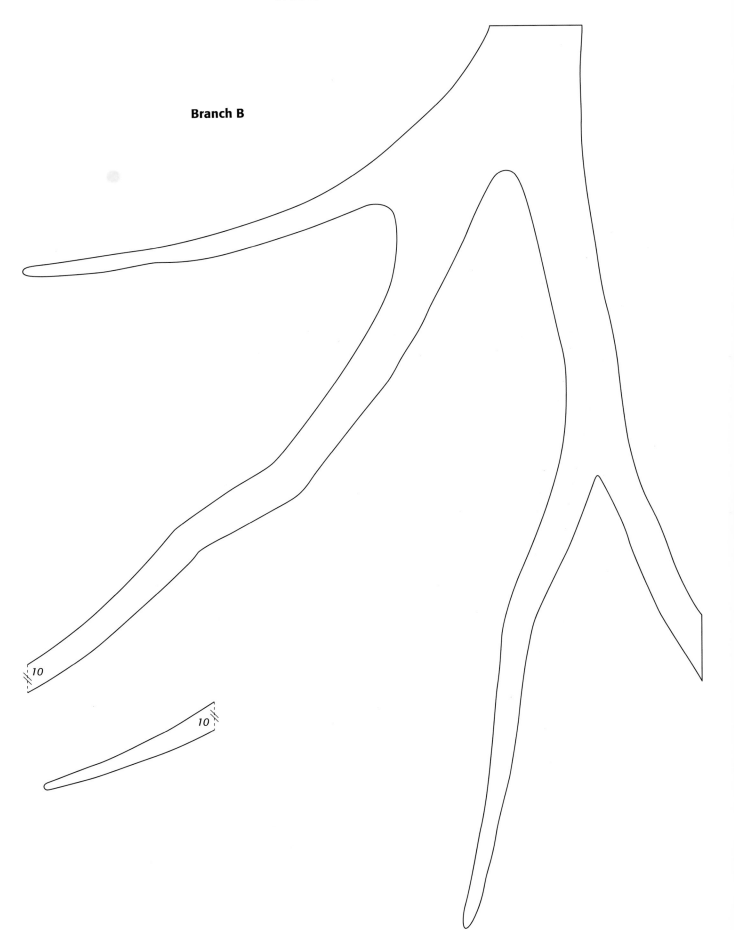

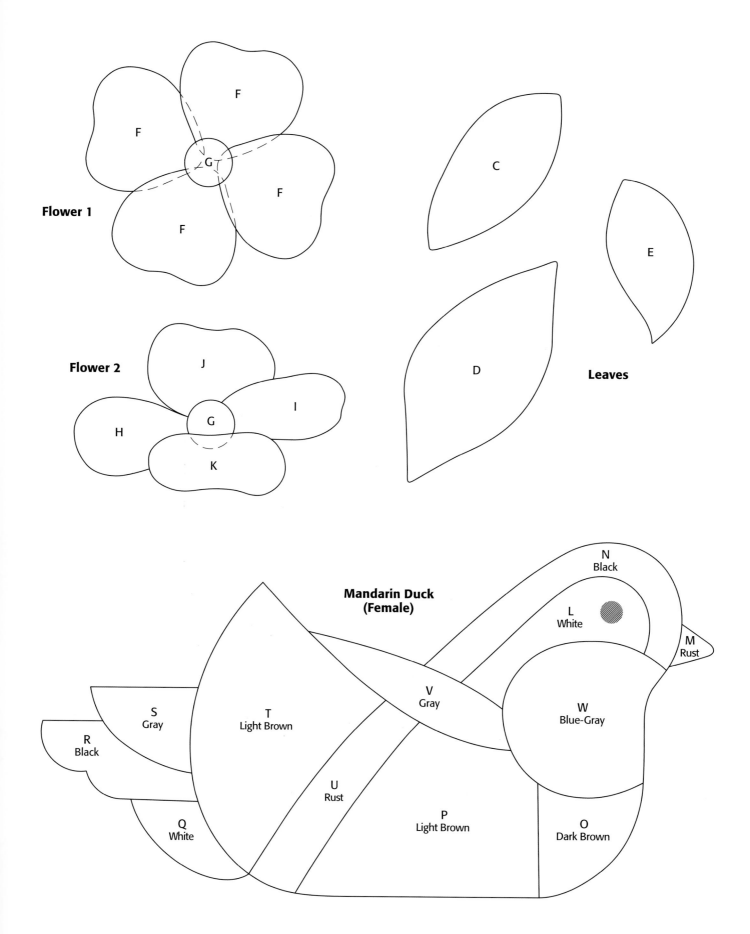

Flower 1

F
F
F
F
G

Flower 2

J
I
H
G
K

C

E

D

Leaves

Mandarin Duck (Female)

N
Black

L
White

M
Rust

V
Gray

W
Blue-Gray

S
Gray

T
Light Brown

R
Black

U
Rust

P
Light Brown

O
Dark Brown

Q
White

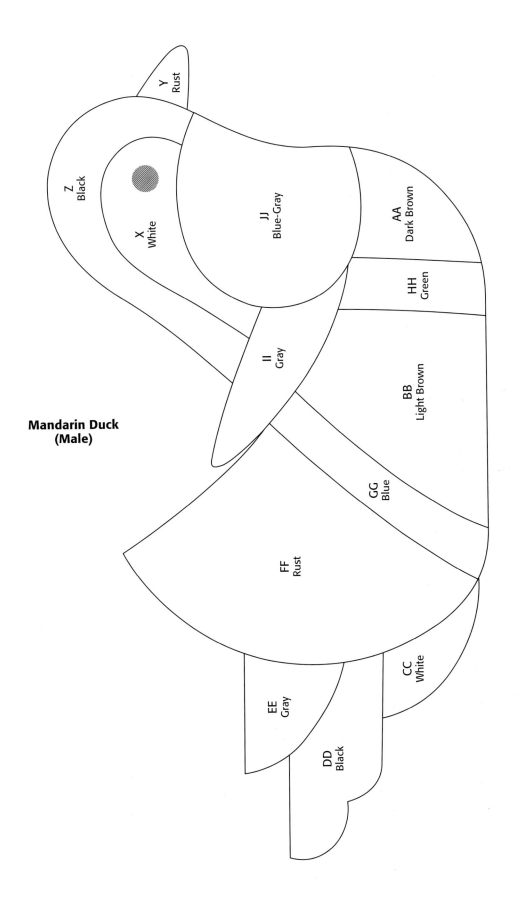

Mandarin Duck (Male)

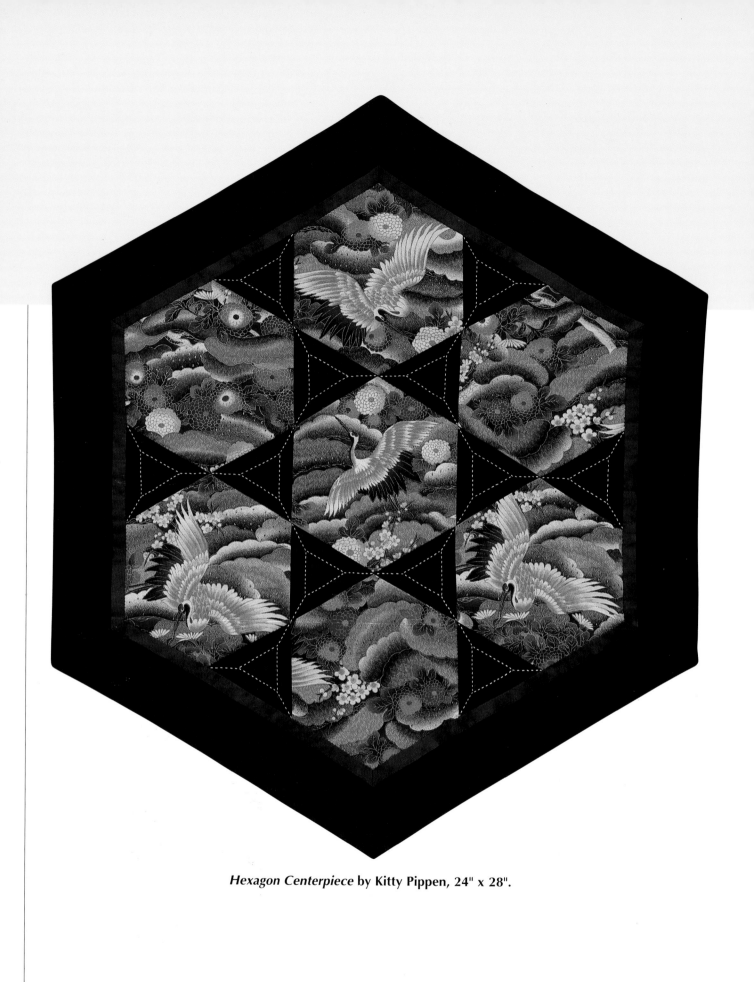

Hexagon Centerpiece by Kitty Pippen, 24" x 28".

Hexagon Centerpiece

Six-inch hexagon shapes accommodate large-scale prints and fit together perfectly with equilateral triangles. The hexagons, cut from an American-made Japanese print fabric, were sewn to the triangles by machine. A simple sashiko design decorates the triangles.

Finished Quilt Size: 24⅞" x 28⅝"

MATERIALS

Yardage is based on 42"-wide fabric.
- ¾ yard of black solid for triangles, outer border, and binding
- ½ yard of print fabric for hexagons
- ¼ yard of bright solid for inner border
- 1 yard of fabric for backing
- 28" x 32" piece of low-loft batting
- 2 sheets of 8½" x 11" template plastic
- White chalk pencil
- Sashiko needle or any sharp needle with a large eye
- White sashiko or #8 perle cotton thread

CUTTING

All measurements include ¼"-wide seam allowances.

From the bright solid, cut:
   6 strips, 1" x 15"

From the black solid, cut:
   6 strips, 2½" x 15"
   3 strips, 2" x 42"

From the backing fabric, cut:
   1 piece, 28" x 32"

ASSEMBLING THE QUILT TOP

1. Trace patterns A, B, and C on pages 63–65 onto template plastic and cut out.
2. Using the templates and the white chalk pencil, trace 7 template A hexagons onto the right side of the print fabric and 12 template B triangles onto the right side of the black solid fabric. Cut out the pieces on the drawn lines. Do not add seam allowance.
3. Stitch the B triangles to the A hexagons as shown to make two outer rows and one center row.

Outer Row
Make 2.

Center Row
Make 1.

4. Arrange the rows as shown and stitch them together.

5. Press the quilt top. Trim the edges if necessary to straighten them.

6. Sew a 1" x 15" inner-border strip to each 2½" x 15" outer-border strip. Press the seam toward the inner-border strip. Fold the strip in half crosswise, wrong sides together. Center template C over each pieced strip, aligning the fold of the strip with the template straight end. Trim the strip end to match the template.

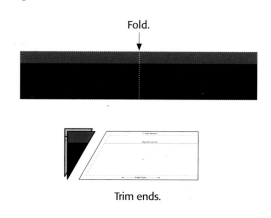

Trim ends.

7. Mark the center point of each border strip and quilt edge. Matching center points, stitch a border strip to each side of the quilt top,

beginning and ending ¼" from each end point. When all of the border strips have been added, stitch the border ends together to create a mitered seam. Press the mitered seams open. Press the inner-border seams toward the border strips.

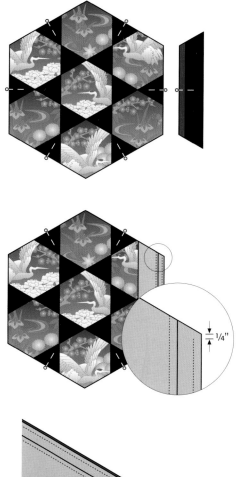

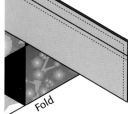

8. Press the quilt top.

9. Refer to "Sashiko" on page 23 to trace the sashiko pattern on page 65 onto each triangle, using the white chalk pencil. Thread a sashiko or other large-eye needle with white sashiko or #8 perle cotton thread. Work the marked design. Press the quilt top from the back.

FINISHING

Refer to "Finishing Techniques" on pages 26–28.

1. Layer the quilt top with batting and backing; baste.

2. Quilt in the ditch around each hexagon and along each border seam.

3. Use the black 2" x 42" strips to bind the quilt edges, binding every other edge first.

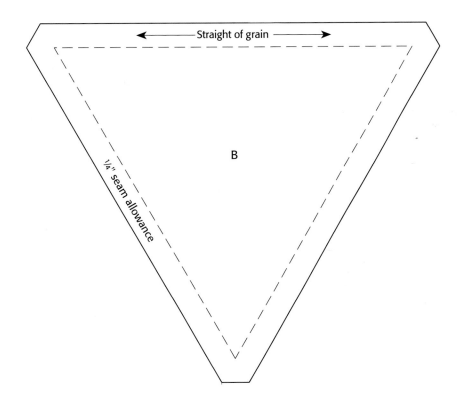

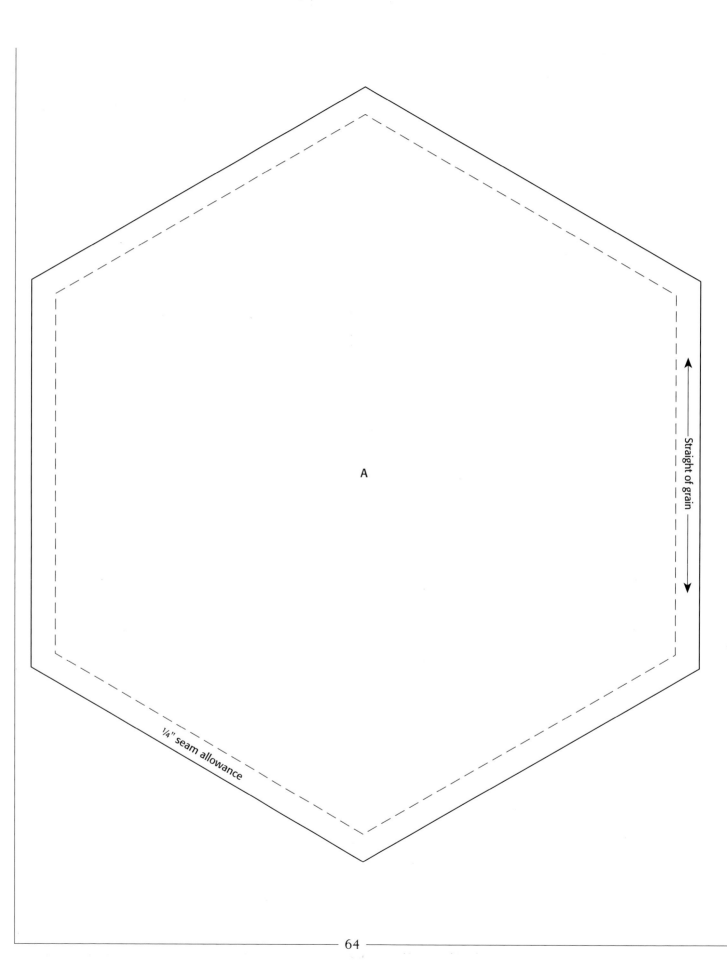

A

Straight of grain

¼" seam allowance

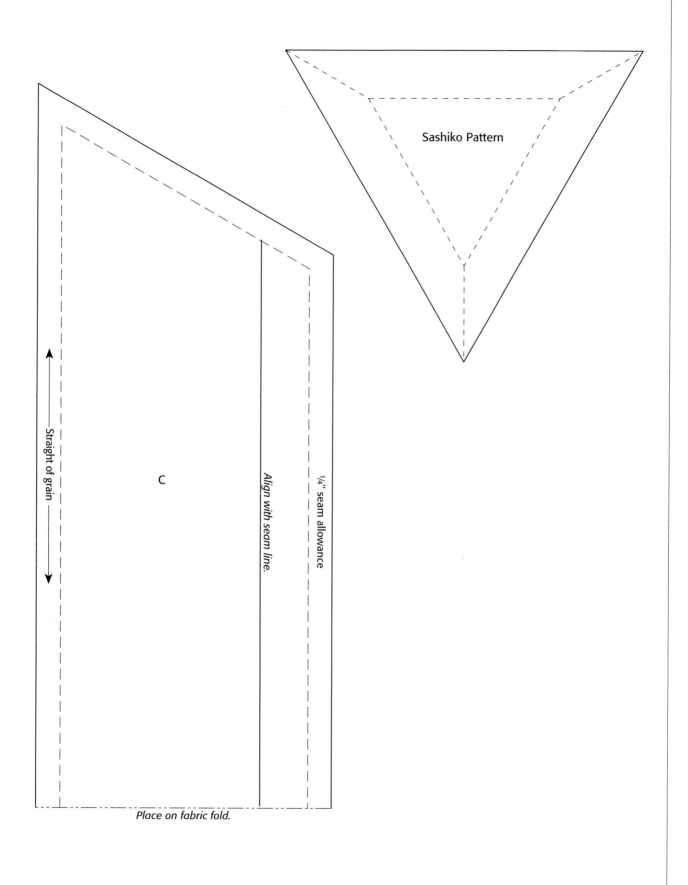

Sashiko Pattern

C

Straight of grain

Align with seam line.

¹/₄" seam allowance

Place on fabric fold.

Hawaiian Panel by Kitty Pippen, 17" x 22".

Hawaiian Panel

As in traditional Hawaiian quilts, this little batik snowflake was cut and appliquéd to a light background and echo quilted.

Finished Quilt Size: 17" x 25"

MATERIALS

Yardage is based on 42"-wide fabric.
- ¾ yard of multicolor batik for appliqués and binding
- ⅝ yard of white solid for background
- ¾ yard of fabric for backing
- 20" x 28" piece of low-loft batting
- 1 sheet of typing paper
- 1 yard of 18"-wide freezer paper
- Fine-line ink pen
- Paper scissors

CUTTING

All measurements include ¼"-wide seam allowances.

From the white solid, cut:
1 rectangle, 17" x 25"

From the multicolor batik, cut:
1 rectangle, 17" x 25"
3 strips, 2" x 42"

From the backing fabric, cut:
1 rectangle, 20" x 28"

PREPARING THE APPLIQUÉS

1. Trace paper-cutting patterns A and B on page 69 onto typing paper and cut out.

2. From the freezer paper, cut one 12" square and one 8" x 12" rectangle. With the dull side down, fold the square as shown. Position pattern A over the folded square and trace around it. Cut out the freezer-paper pattern. Repeat to fold the rectangle and trace and cut out pattern B as shown.

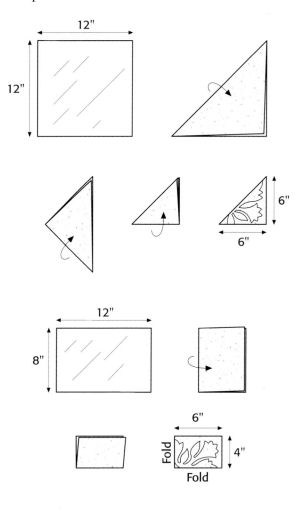

3. Unfold the freezer-paper patterns and carefully position them, shiny side down, on the right side of the batik rectangle, leaving an equal amount of space at the top and bottom and an equal amount on each side.

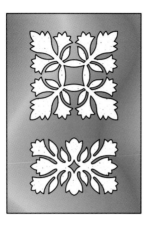

4. With the pen, draw around both patterns. This line will be turned under and hidden when the pieces are appliquéd in place.

APPLIQUÉING

1. With the right side up, place the marked batik rectangle over the background rectangle, aligning all of the edges; pin the corners together.
2. Remove the freezer-paper patterns. Hand or machine baste inside each shape, approximately ¼" from the marked lines. Cut away the batik fabric ⅛" beyond the marked line of one motif for several inches. Refer to "Needle-Turn Method" on page 21 to appliqué this small section, making sure the pen line is turned under. Continue cutting and appliquéing small sections until the entire motif is appliquéd. The fabric will fray less if you work in short sections.

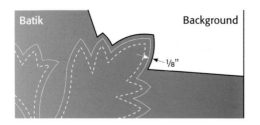

Cut ⅛" beyond pattern line.

3. Repeat step 2 to appliqué the remaining motif.
4. Press the quilt top from the wrong side.

FINISHING

Refer to "Finishing Techniques" on pages 26–28.

1. Layer the quilt top with batting and backing; baste.
2. Using white thread, quilt in the ditch around each motif. Echo quilt the remaining background, spacing the rows ¼" apart.

3. Press the quilt from the front and back.
4. Use the batik strips to bind the quilt edges.

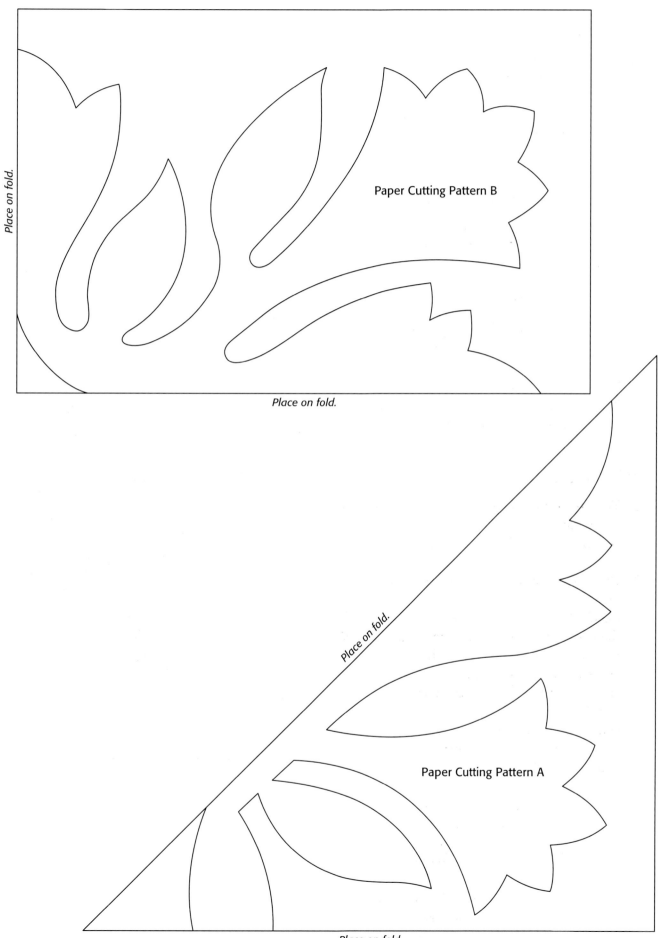

Place on fold.

Paper Cutting Pattern B

Place on fold.

Place on fold.

Paper Cutting Pattern A

Place on fold.

Tahitian Hibiscus **by Sylvia Pippen, 26½" x 31½".**

Tahitian Hibiscus

Hibiscus is another symbol of the tropics and is featured on many textiles and quilts throughout the Pacific Islands. This quilt is a simplified variation of a tifaifai quilt from the Cook Islands. The batik petals and stamens are needle-turn appliquéd and the background appliqué leaf pattern is outlined in gold sashiko.

Finished Quilt Size: 27" x 32"

MATERIALS

Yardage is based on 42"-wide fabric.
- 1 yard of deep red fabric for background
- 1 yard of green fabric for leaf motifs and binding
- Scraps of assorted yellow and pink batiks for flowers
- 1 yard of fabric for backing
- 29" x 34" piece of low-loft batting
- Several sheets of typing paper
- White chalk pencil
- Japanese sashiko needle or any sharp needle with a large eye
- Yellow or gold sashiko thread or #8 perle cotton

CUTTING

All measurements include ¼"-wide seam allowances.

From the deep red fabric, cut:
   1 rectangle, 27" x 32"

From the green fabric, cut:
   4 strips, 2" x 42"

From the backing fabric, cut:
   1 rectangle, 29" x 34"

APPLIQUÉING THE QUILT TOP

1. Using a photocopy machine, enlarge patterns A, B, and C on pages 73 and 74 by the percentage indicated. Make one enlarged A shape and two each of B and C. Trace patterns D–I on page 75 onto typing paper, four times each. Cut out the shapes. Mark the letter on the front of each piece.

2. Referring to "Needle-Turn Method" on page 21, pin the A, B, and C paper pieces to the *wrong* side of the remaining green fabric. Pin pieces D–I to the *right* side of the appropriate assorted pink and yellow batik fabrics. Cut out each shape, adding a generous ⅛" seam allowance all around.

3. Fold the red background rectangle into fourths to determine the center point. Using the chalk pencil, mark diagonal lines from corner to corner, through the center point. These intersecting lines will help you to place the leaf patterns accurately.

4. Position appliqué A diagonally over the center and pin baste in place. Place appliqués B and C around A as shown and pin baste in place. Appliqué the leaves in place using matching green thread. Appliqué the flower petals and stamens over the leaves as shown, working in alphabetical order and using matching thread.

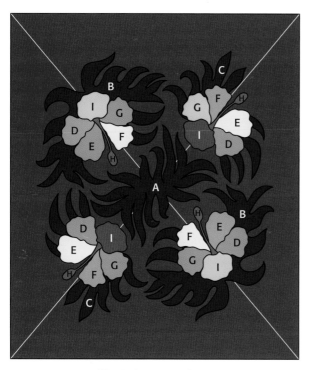

Appliqué Placement Diagram

5. Press the appliquéd rectangle from the back.
6. Referring to "Sashiko" on page 23, work sashiko around all the leaves, using yellow or gold thread.

FINISHING

Refer to "Finishing Techniques" on pages 26–28.

1. Layer the quilt top with batting and backing; baste.
2. Using thread that matches the background fabric, quilt in the ditch around the flowers. Stitch close to the sashiko around all of the leaves. Quilt diagonal lines in the background.

3. Use the green strips to bind the quilt.

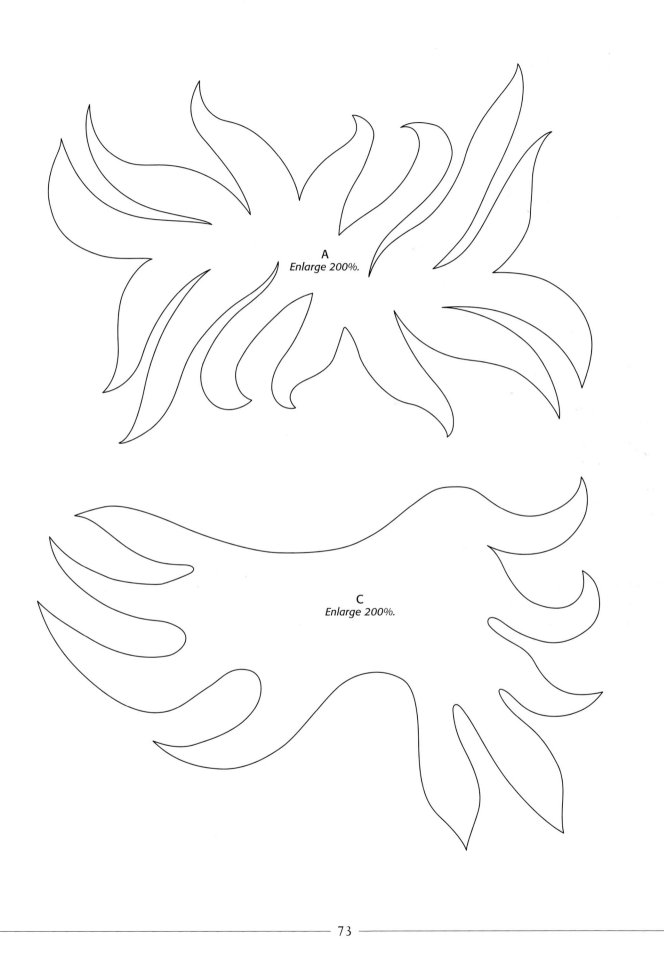

A
Enlarge 200%.

C
Enlarge 200%.

B
Enlarge 200%.

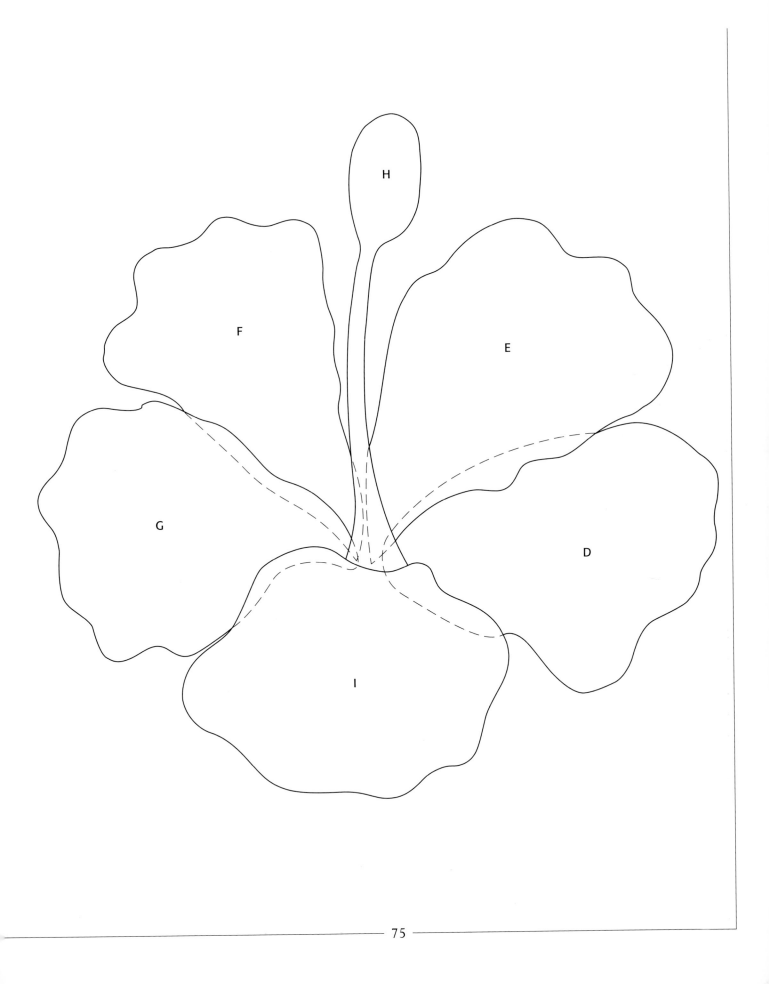

Scrappy Hawaiian by Sylvia Pippen, 37" x 49".

Scrappy Hawaiian

The blocks in this quilt are pieced from bold pareu prints. Pareu is a French Polynesian name for a body wrap. These fabrics are widely used throughout Polynesia for daily clothing and hula costumes. If you have scraps of Hawaiian fabric or Japanese yukatas, this would be an ideal design for using them. Mix them up with your stash of solids and batiks to make the two-fabric blocks.

Finished Quilt Size: 38½" x 50½"

MATERIALS

Yardage is based on 42"-wide fabric.
- ¼ yard *each* of 8 assorted large-scale Hawaiian floral prints for blocks
- ¼ yard *each* of 8 assorted solids or batiks for blocks
- ½ yard of wide (5") Hawaiian border print or large-scale floral for border
- ½ yard of solid-color fabric that coordinates with border print for border
- ⅜ yard of narrow (3") Hawaiian border print or large-scale floral for border
- 1⅝ yards of fabric for backing
- ½ yard of coordinating solid fabric for binding
- 40" x 52" piece of low-loft batting
- One 8½" x 11" sheet of template plastic
- Fine-line permanent ink pen
- ¼" presser foot (optional)

CUTTING

All measurements include ¼"-wide seam allowances.

From the wide Hawaiian border print or floral, cut:
2 strips, 5½" x 24½"

From the narrow Hawaiian border print, cut:
2 strips, 3½" x 24½"

From the coordinating solid for border, cut:
1 strip, 5½" x 18½"
1 strip, 5½" x 14½"
1 strip, 3½" x 18½"
1 strip, 3½" x 14½"

From the backing fabric, cut:
1 rectangle, 40" x 52"

From the coordinating solid for binding, cut:
5 strips, 2" x 42"

ASSEMBLING THE QUILT TOP

1. Trace patterns A and B on pages 80 and 81 onto template plastic. Be sure to mark the alignment dots. Cut out the templates.

2. Using template A and the ink pen, trace 35 shapes onto the right side of the Hawaiian floral prints. Cut out the pieces on the marked lines. In the same manner, use template B to make 35 shapes from the solids and batiks.

3. With wrong sides together, align the concave curve of each B piece with the convex curve of an A piece. Pin the pieces together at the center alignment dots first, then at the corners, and finally at the dots between the corner and center dots, easing in any fullness.

4. Stitch ¼" from the curved edges through the marked dots, using the ¼" presser foot if desired. Press the seam allowance toward piece B. Make 35 blocks.

5. Arrange the blocks in seven rows of five blocks each as shown. Sew the blocks in each row together. Press the seams in opposite directions from row to row. Sew the rows together. Trim the edges, if necessary, to straighten and square up the quilt top.

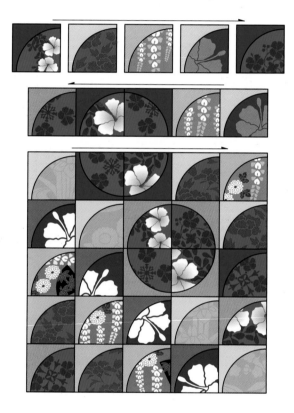

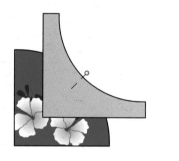

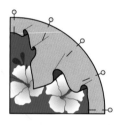

6. Stitch the border pieces together as shown. Sew the side borders to the quilt sides. Stitch the top and bottom borders to the top and bottom edges.

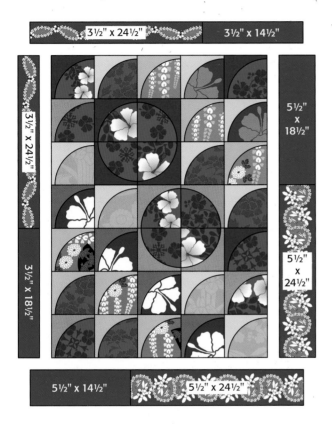

Variation

Scrappy Yukata
by Kitty Pippen, 35" x 38".

This quilt is just what the name implies and is a good way to salvage small scraps of beautiful fabric.

FINISHING

Refer to "Finishing Techniques" on pages 26–28.

1. Layer the quilt top with batting and backing; baste.
2. Quilt in the ditch around the blocks and curved seams.
3. Add a hanging sleeve. Bind the quilt edges.

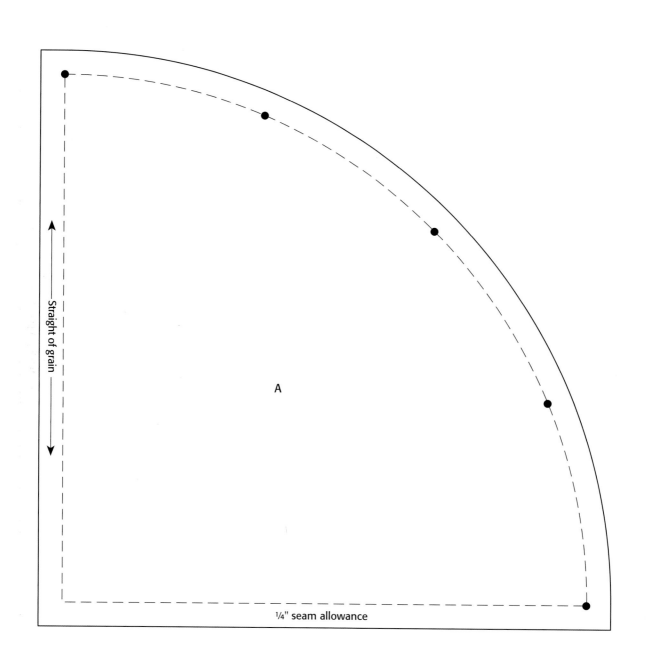

Straight of grain

A

¼" seam allowance

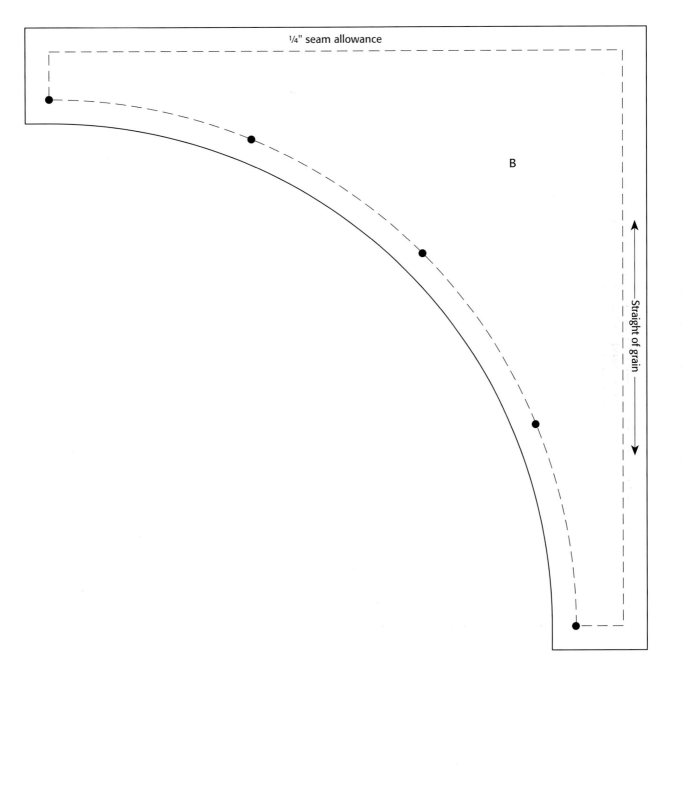

¼" seam allowance

B

Straight of grain

Heliconia by Sylvia Pippen, 20" x 27".

Heliconia

This quilt is a smaller, appliquéd version of "Heliconia with Bamboo" (page 86). I used a blue, cotton sateen background and a sunset batik for the border. The paper-piecing method of appliqué was used to form the heliconia petals. Sashiko creates the outline of bamboo in the background.

Finished Quilt Size: 23½" x 30½"

MATERIALS

Yardage is based on 42"-wide fabric.
- 1 yard of multicolor batik for outer border and binding
- ½ yard of gradated medium-to-dark blue solid for background
- ¼ yard of gradated pink-to-red solid for inner border
- 1 fat quarter of purplish-pink batik for stems
- Scraps of assorted pink and yellow batiks for flower petals
- Scraps of 3 assorted green fabrics with linear design for bamboo leaves
- 1 yard of fabric for backing
- 26" x 33" piece of low-loft batting
- Design-transfer materials
- One 8½" x 11" sheet of template plastic
- Fine-tip permanent ink pen
- Japanese sashiko needle or any sharp needle with a large eye
- White sashiko thread or #8 perle cotton

CUTTING

All measurements include ¼"-wide seam allowances.

From the gradated medium-to-dark blue solid, cut:
  1 rectangle, 16" x 23"

From the purplish-pink batik, cut:
  2 bias strips, ⅝" x 12"

From gradated pink-to-red solid, cut:
  2 strips, 1" x 22"
  2 strips, 1" x 16½"

From the multicolor batik, cut:
  4 strips, 4" x 23½"
  3 strips, 2" x 42"

From the backing fabric, cut:
  1 rectangle, 26" x 33"

PREPARING THE BACKGROUND

1. Using a photocopy machine, enlarge the pattern on page 86 by the percentage indicated.
2. Center the enlarged pattern over the right side of the background rectangle. Transfer the flower, stem, and leaf motifs to the fabric, using your favorite method. The bamboo lines will be marked after the appliqués are stitched in place.

PREPARING THE APPLIQUÉS

1. Trace appliqué patterns A–Q on page 87 onto template plastic. Cut out the templates.
2. Using the ink pen and templates A–E and J–Q, trace the petal and bud shapes onto the right side of the assorted pink and yellow batik scraps as follows:

Template	Number to Cut
A	3 and 1 reversed
B	2 and 6 reversed
C	2 and 2 reversed
D	1 and 3 reversed
E	3
J–Q	1 each

3. Using templates F–I, trace the leaf shapes onto the right sides of the assorted green fabrics as follows:

Template	Number to Cut
F	1 and 1 reversed
G	2 and 1 reversed
H	4
I	1 and 2 reversed

4. Cut out the petals, bud pieces, and leaves, adding ⅛" seam allowance around each shape.

APPLIQUÉING THE QUILT TOP

1. Fold each purplish-pink stem strip in thirds lengthwise, slightly overlapping the raw edges in the center of each strip as shown. Press; then baste each strip through the center, stitching through all the layers.

2. Lay one edge of each bias strip on the marked stem line of the background rectangle, leaving enough stem length at each end to hide beneath the buds and leaves; pin in place. Referring to "Traditional Appliqué Stitch" on page 22, appliqué the strip along the right edge, shaping the strip around the curves as you stitch. Leave the left edge unstitched until the petals have been appliquéd in place.

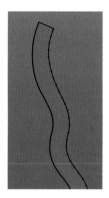

Stitch along right edge of stems.
Leave left edge unstitched.

3. Referring to the pattern, appliqué the petals (A–E) in place. Position the petals shown on the right edge of the stem so they overlap the stitched edge slightly. Place the petals shown on the left edge of the stem so they will be just under the strip edge when it is appliquéd in place. Appliqué the left edge of the stem strip in place.
4. Working in alphabetical order, appliqué the leaves (F–I) in place, referring to the pattern for placement. Tuck the stem ends under the G leaves where indicated.

5. Appliqué the bud pieces in place as shown, working in alphabetical order.

6. Press the quilt top from the wrong side.

EMBELLISHING THE BACKGROUND AND ADDING BORDERS

1. Lay the quilt top over the enlarged pattern and transfer the bamboo lines to the rectangle.

2. Referring to "Sashiko" on page 23, work sashiko along the bamboo lines, using the white thread.

3. Trim the quilt top to 15" x 22", keeping the design centered.

4. Stitch the 1" x 22" pink-to-red strips to the quilt sides. Press the seams toward the borders. Stitch the 1" x 16½" pink-to-red strips to the top and bottom edges of the quilt top. Press the seams toward the borders. In the same manner, stitch the 4" x 23½" multi-color batik strips to the quilt side and then the top and bottom edges. Press the seams toward the borders.

FINISHING

Refer to "Finishing Techniques" on pages 26–28.

1. Layer the quilt top with batting and backing; baste.

2. Using thread that matches the background fabric, quilt in the ditch around the appliquéd flowers, buds, leaves, and stems. To emphasize the bamboo design, quilt along the sashiko lines.

3. Add a hanging sleeve. Bind the quilt edges.

Enlarge 250%.

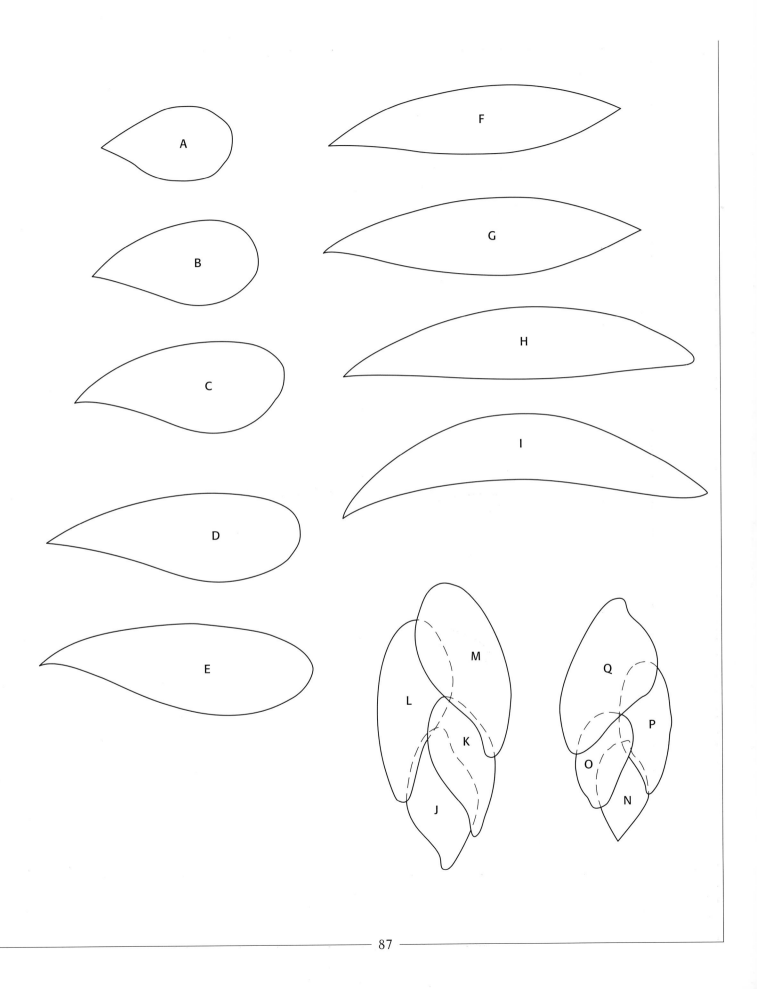

Sashiko Designs

**Sashiko Patterns
(Family Crests)**
*Reduce or enlarge
to desired size.*

Gentian

Wood Sorrel

Mandarin Orange Flower

Paulownia

Cherry Blossom

Plum Blossom

Ginkgo Leaf Patterns
*Reduce or enlarge
to desired size.*

Ginkgo Leaf Patterns
*Reduce or enlarge
to desired size.*

Quilting Designs

Kauai Turtleback

Shell

Hawaiian Quilting Designs
Enlarge to desired size.

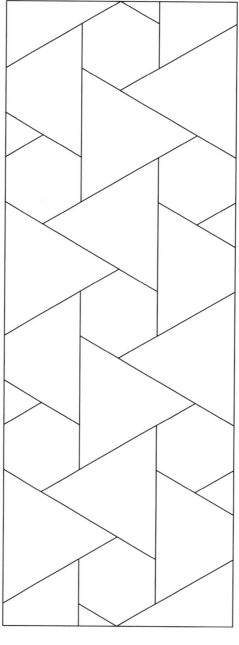

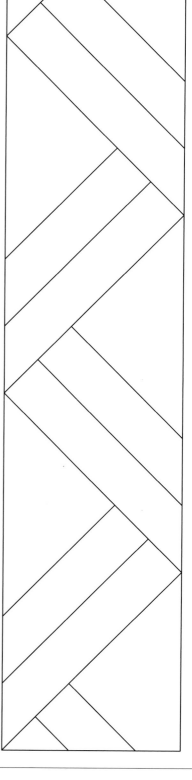

Quilting Patterns for Borders
Reduce or enlarge to desired size.

Quilting Pattern for Water
Reduce or enlarge to desired size.

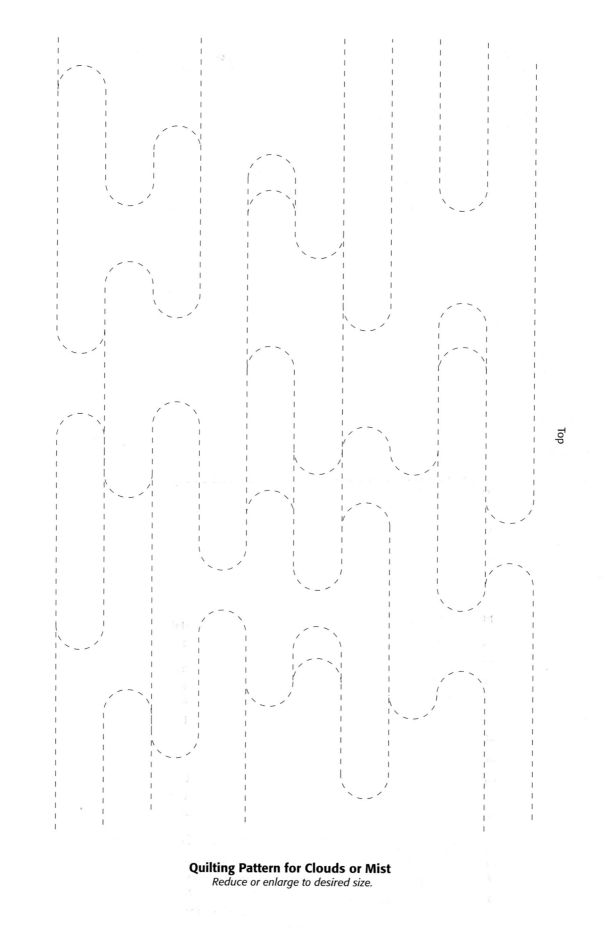

Top

Quilting Pattern for Clouds or Mist
Reduce or enlarge to desired size.

Bibliography

Bryant, Claire. *Tropical Flowers: Iron-On Transfer Patterns.* New York: Dover Publications, Inc., 1992.

Hammond, Joyce D. *Tifaifai and the Quilts of Polynesia.* Honolulu, Hawaii: University of Hawaii Press, 1986.
A scholarly description of the history of Polynesian quilts.

Hope, Dale, with Gregory Tozian. *The Aloha Shirt: Spirit of the Islands.* Hillsboro, Oreg.: Beyond Words Publishing, 2000.

Matsuya Piece Goods Store. Translated by Fumi Adachi. *Japanese Design Motifs with 4260 Illustrations of Heraldic Crests.* New York: Dover Publications, Inc., 1972.
Invaluable source for sashiko or appliqué designs.

Mende, Kazuko, and Reiko Morishige. *Sashiko, Blue and White Quilt Art of Japan.* Tokyo: Kodansha America, Inc., 1991.

Nakano, Eisha, and Barbara B. Stephan. *Japanese Stencil Dyeing.* New York and Tokyo: John Weatherhill, Inc., 1982.
Paste-resist techniques.

Nihon Vogue. *Sashiko.* Tokyo: Nihon Vogue Publishing Co., Ltd., 1989.

Ouchi, Hajime. *Japanese Optical and Geometric Art.* New York: Dover Publications, Inc., 1977.

Rongokea, Lynnsay, and John Daley. *The Art of Tivaevae: Traditional Cook Islands Quilting.* Honolulu, Hawaii: University of Hawaii Press, 2001.
Beautiful photography of Island women and their quilts.

Shaw, Robert. *Hawaiian Quilt Masterpieces.* Hugh Lauter Levin Associates, Inc., 1996.

Venters, Diana, and Elaine Krajenke Ellison. *Mathematical Quilts.* Emeryville, Calif.: Key Curriculum Press, 1999.

Yang, Sunny, and Rochelle M. Narasin. *Textile Art of Japan.* Tokyo: Shufunotomo Co., Ltd., 1989.
Richly illustrated with much information about the techniques of dyeing, weaving, and needlework.

Resources

Barkcloth Hawaii
www.barkclothhawaii.com

Eastwind Art
PO Box 811
Sebastopol, CA 95473
707-829-3536 (phone)
www.eastwindart.com
Japanese-style patterns, fabrics, stencils, books, gifts

Honey Run Quilter
1230 Esplanade
Chico, CA 95926
530-342-5464

Kapaia Stitchery
Julie Yakamuri
PO Box 1327
Lihue, Kauai, HI 96766
808-245-2281
Hawaiian fabrics, quilts, and patterns

Katsuri Dye Works
Koji and Debby Wada
PO Box 1448
Saratoga, WY 82331
888-841-6997

Marjorie Lee Bevis
1401 Oakwood Drive
Oakland, OR 97462
541-459-1921
www.marbledfabrics.com
Marbled fabrics and accessories

Mountain Maid Quilter
135 Main Street
Chester, CA 96020
530-258-3901

Petroglyph
Wendy Lee
PO Box 7323
Menlo Park, CA 94025
650-851-0434

Thousand Cranes Futon Shop
1803 Fourth Avenue
Berkeley, CA 94710
510-849-0501
Imported fabrics

About the Authors

Sylvia Pippen at the age of four.

KITTY PIPPEN (above, at right) was born November 18, 1919, at Ping Ting Chow, Shansi, China, where her parents were missionaries. Her appreciation of fine needlework comes from spending many childhood hours watching the Chinese women mend and quilt their clothing and do embroidery. Kitty, her twin sister, and her brother were schooled at home before attending an American high school near Bejing. After coming to the United States for college, Kitty married and moved to California, where she and her husband raised their family.

For many years, Kitty worked as a draftsperson in the biochemistry department at the University of California, Berkeley. During this time, Kitty discovered Japanese fabric, and after retiring to Lake Almanor, she made her first Japanese quilt. Since then, she has been lecturing, teaching, and sharing her love of Japanese textiles.

SYLVIA PIPPEN (above and far left) was born into a family of artists and musicians in 1948 and grew up in the San Francisco Bay Area where she studied classical flute. Her mother, Kitty, taught her to sew at a very early age and imprinted a life-long passion for fabric upon her.

While raising her family in Shelburne Falls, Massachusetts, Sylvia studied tailoring and pattern making, and designed jackets made with yukatas and Seminole patchwork. Owner of a perennial flower nursery, Sylvia designed and installed gardens and wrote weekly gardening columns for the local newspaper.

Sylvia developed her style of quilting when she moved to Kauai and worked as a gardener among tropical exotics. While crewing on sailboats, she discovered the joy of appliqué, perfect for small quarters. She haunted the local quilt store and started making quilts inspired by the fabric and images of the Islands. Sylvia also is a flute teacher and registered nurse when she is not in the garden or quilting.